Help Me Handle This!

Dr. John R. Adolph

This book is dedicated to Jesus Christ and His finished work on the cross.

To devout believers in the Lord whose human doubt, dismay, and disbelief demands and necessitates the cross of Christ and the grace of God.

To sincere followers of Jesus Christ who have been hit, hurt, hindered, harmed, and hampered by some of life's most challenging conditions and circumstances yet have remained faithful.

To active Sunday morning worshippers who sometimes struggle while being tested.

To in-active church members around the world who have wanted to quit and give up on God because they have had moments where they have felt like God abandoned them when they needed Him the most.

To Pastors who preach the faith to empower others but need encouragement themselves from time to time.

To every real Christian who can openly admit that without God's grace, you would be nothing, but with God's strength, we can endure, persevere and conquer any life challenges that come our way.

HELP ME Handle This!

Spiritual Truth That Empowers the Faithful to Persevere and Overcome

Dr. JOHN R. ADOLPH

HELP ME HANDLE THIS by Dr. John R. Adolph
Copyright © 2023 by John R. Adolph
All Rights Reserved.
ISBN: 978-1-59755-828-0

Published by: ADVANTAGE BOOKS™, Orlando, FL
                www.advbookstore.com

All Rights Reserved. This book and parts thereof may not be reproduced in any form, stored in a retrieval system or transmitted in any form by any means (electronic, mechanical, photocopy, recording or otherwise) without prior written permission of the author, except as provided by United States of America copyright law.
Scriptures quotations taken from the Holy Bible KING JAMES VERSION (KJV), public domain.

Library of Congress Catalog Number: 2024950667

Name:	Adolph, John R., Author
Title:	***HELP ME HANDLE THIS***
	John R. Adolph
	Advantage Books, 2024
Identifiers:	ISBN Paperback: 9781597558280
	ISBN eBook: 9781597558365
Subjects:	Books › Religion & Spirituality › Worship & Devotion Devotionals
	Books › Religion & Spirituality › Worship & Devotion Inspirational
	Books › Religion & Spirituality › Worship & Devotion Prayer

First Printing: December 2024
24 25 26 27 28 29 30   10 9 8 7 6 5 4 3 2 1

Table of Contents

ACKNOWLEDGEMENTS 9

INTRODUCTION 11

Week 1: Help Me Handle My Brand New Start (Isaiah 43:19)
Day 1: DO NOT EXPECT A REPEAT! 13
Day 2: GOD SAID, 'FORGET IT!' 15
Day 3: NEW LOOKS GOOD ON YOU! 16
Day 4: IT'S COMING! 17
Day 5: YOUR GOD IS A WAY MAKER! 18
Day 6: EXPECT THE IMPOSSIBLE! 19
Day 7: THIS IS THE MOMENT YOU HAVE BEEN WAITING FOR! 20

Week 2: Help Me Handle The Company I Keep (Psalms 1:1)
Day 1: GOD CHOOSES YOUR FAMILY BUT YOU PICK YOUR FRIENDS! 21
Day 2: YOU SHOULD BLESS YOURSELF! 23
Day 3: RUN FROM BAD ADVICE! 24
Day 4: STAND FOR SOMETHING OR FALL FOR ANYTHING! 25
Day 5: BAD COMPANY CORRUPTS GOOD MANNERS! 26
Day 6: WITH THE WRONG PEOPLE IN YOUR LIFE, THINGS CAN GO FROM BAD TO WORSE! 27
Day 7: SOME PEOPLE YOU CUT AND OTHERS YOU KEEP! 28

Week 3: Help Me Handle This Bank Account Of Mine (1 Kings 17:15-16)
Day 1: YOU ARE NOT SUPPOSED TO BE BROKE! 29
Day 2: God's Word For You Today: GOD WILL PROVIDE! 31
Day 3: LITTLE BECOMES MUCH WHEN USED THE RIGHT WAY! 32
Day 4: OBEDIENCE AND OVERFLOW ARE ALWAYS EQUALS! 33
Day 5: WHAT YOU HAVE NOW IS NOT ALL GOD WANTS YOU TO POSSESS! ... 34
Day 6: God's Word For You Today: THE FLOOD GATES ARE NOW OPEN! 35
Day 7: God's Word For You Today: THE CHOICE IS YOURS! 36

Week 4: Help Me Handle How I Feel (Galatians 6:9)
Day 1: YOUR DUE SEASON IS NOW DUE! 37
Day 2: DON'T QUIT! 39
Day 3: YOU'RE NOT ALONE! 40
Day 4: THERE'S A REASON FOR YOUR SEASON! 41
Day 5: DON'T LET BEING TIRED TAKE YOU OUT! 42

DAY 6: KEEP DOING THE RIGHT THING! 43
DAY 7: IT'S MY CHOICE! 44

Week 5: Help Me Handle It When There's Somebody For Everybody But Me (2 Cor. 6:14)
DAY 1: DIFFERENT LEVELS CAN EXPOSE NEW DEVILS! 45
DAY 2: DON'T IGNORE THE WARNING SIGNS! 46
DAY 3: ASK THEM THIS QUESTION: WHAT DO YOU REALLY BELIEVE? 47
DAY 4: BE CAREFUL TOO MUCH, TOO SOON CAN BE DANGEROUS! 48
DAY 5: IF YOU WALK IN THE LIGHT, WHAT'S DARK WON'T LAST LONG! 49
DAY 6: IF GOD DID NOT SEND YOU, I'M NOT AVAILABLE! 50
DAY 7: TO BE SINGLE DOES NOT MEAN YOU HAVE TO BE LONELY! 51

Week 6: Help Me Handle My Marriage When There's No Wine Left (St. John 2:9-10)
DAY 1: YOUR WINE IS SWEET, SO ENJOY IT WHILE IT LAST! 53
DAY 2: GOD WILL ALLOW YOUR MARRIAGE TO RUN OUT OF WINE! 55
DAY 3: DON'T BE AFRAID TO ADMIT THAT YOUR MARRIAGE NEEDS A REFILL! 56
DAY 4: DON'T LET THE DEVIL HAVE YOUR MARRIAGE! 57
DAY 5: DO WHATEVER IT TAKES! 58
DAY 6: NEW WINE IS ALWAYS THE BEST! 59
DAY 7: IT CAN LAST FOREVER! 61

Week 7: Help Handle It When I'm Sick Of It (1 Samuel 1:9)
DAY 1: CHANGE ISN'T BAD IT IS NECESSARY! 63
DAY 2: GOD'S WORD FOR YOU TODAY: RISE! 64
DAY 3: WHAT'S BITTER WILL SOON BECOME BETTER! 65
DAY 4: PRAY YOUR WAY THROUGH! 66
DAY 5: YESTERDAY I CRIED! 67
DAY 6: I'VE HAD ENOUGH! 68
DAY 7: WATCH GOD CHANGE IT! 69

Week 8: Help Me Handle It When It's Too Much For Me To Handle (St. Matthew 11:28-30)
DAY 1: IF IT'S TOO MUCH FOR YOU, IT'S JUST RIGHT FOR HIM! 71
DAY 2: EVERYONE NEEDS IT, BUT NOT EVERYBODY QUALIFIES! 73
DAY 3: I WILL MEANS HE HEALS! 74
DAY 4: HIS REST IS YOUR GIFT! 75
DAY 5: GOOD NEWS, HE'S CARRYING YOU AND YOUR LOAD! 76
DAY 6: LEARN THE LESSON, LEAVE THE PAIN! 77
DAY 7: GOD WILL TAKE CARE OF YOU! 78

Week 9: Help Me Handle Enemies In Close Proximity (Psalms 23:5)
- DAY 1: GOD SAYS, "I'VE INVITED YOUR ENEMIES!"! 79
- DAY 2: YOUR LIFE IS BEING GUARDED BY THE LORD! 81
- DAY 3: GET OVER IT! 82
- DAY 4: I WANT YOUR ENEMIES TO SEE MY FAVOR ON YOUR LIFE! 83
- DAY 5: YOU'RE AT THE TABLE, BUT YOU DON'T HAVE A TAB! 84
- DAY 6: GRACE WORKS FOR THEM LIKE IT WORKS FOR YOU! 85
- DAY 7: SHOW THEM WHAT OVERFLOW LOOKS LIKE! 86

Week 10 Help Me Handle It When What I Need Is A Refill (Ephesians 5:18)
- DAY 1: PARKED CARS DO NOT NEED MORE GAS FOR THE JOURNEY THAT LIES AHEAD! 87
- DAY 2: BE CAREFUL WHERE YOU GET YOUR REFILL FROM! 88
- DAY 3: IF YOU REALLY NEED A REFILL LEARN TO PARTNER WITH THE RIGHT PEOPLE! 89
- DAY 4: WHAT YOU REALLY NEED IS ANOTHER DOSE OF THE HOLY GHOST! 90
- DAY 5: WHEN YOU'RE FULL YOU OPERATE MUCH BETTER! 91
- DAY 6: BEING EMPTY IS NOT FUNNY, IT'S DANGEROUS! 92
- DAY 7: FILL-UP'S ARE FREE BECAUSE THEY'VE ALREADY BEEN PAID FOR! 93

Week 11: Help Me Handle the Mess I'm In (Genesis 3:10)
- DAY 1: SOMETIMES I HATE THE SHAPE THAT I'M IN, BUT I LOVE THE HOPE THAT I HAVE! 95
- DAY 2: HE KNOWS YOUR SIN, BUT HE CALLS YOU BY YOUR NAME! 97
- DAY 3: YOU ARE NOT THE MESS YOU HAVE MADE! 98
- DAY 4: WHY ARE YOU WHERE YOU ARE? 99
- DAY 5: HE'S GOT A MASTER PLAN! 100
- DAY 6: HE COVERS YOU SO THAT HE CAN REDEEM YOU! 101
- DAY 7: WHAT YOU DON'T HAVE GRACE WILL PROVIDE! 102

Week 12: Help Me Handle My Losses (Job 1:20-22)
- DAY 1: IT'S A TEST, SO DON'T LET GOD DOWN! 103
- DAY 2: REMEMBER THAT YOU AND EVERYTHING YOU OWN IS GOD'S PROPERTY! 105
- DAY 3: REALIZE THAT GOD'S GOODNESS IS YOUR POSSESSION! 106
- DAY 4: IT'S NOT JUST WHAT HE TOOK, IT'S WHAT HE LET YOU KEEP! 107
- DAY 5: LET GO AND HOLD ON! 108
- DAY 6: THEIR ABSENCE HURT, BUT HIS PRESENCE HEALS! 109
- DAY 7: GOD'S PRAISE IS YOUR PURPOSE 110

Week 13: Help Me Handle Satanic Attacks Launched Against Me (St. Luke 22:31-32)
- Day 1: GOD IS STILL IN CONTROL! 111
- Day 2: THE LORD COULD HAVE STOPPED IT BUT HE DIDN'T! 113
- Day 3: IF THE DEVIL COULD HAVE IT HIS WAY, YOUR LIFE WOULD BE BROKEN INTO PIECES!... 114
- Day 4: HE'S TURNING IT AROUND JUST FOR YOU! 115
- Day 5: DON'T LET ANYTHING OR ANYBODY SEPARATE YOU FROM YOU! 116
- Day 6: NOW THAT YOU HAVE MADE IT HELP SOMEBODY ELSE GET THROUGH! 117
- Day 7: NEVER FORGET THIS: HE'S PREPARING YOU! 119

Week 14: Help Me Handle How I Treat Him (St. Mark 14:2)
- Day 1: GOD WANTS YOUR VERY BEST! 121
- Day 2: YOU OWE HIM AND YOU KNOW IT! 123
- Day 3: PREPARE TO BE CRITICIZED! 125
- Day 4: TREAT HIM LIKE A KING! 127
- Day 5: YOU'RE DOING IT RIGHT WHEN……! 129
- Day 6: DO IT BECAUSE YOU CAN! 131
- Day 7: WHAT HE DESERVES IS A WORSHIP THAT'S REAL! 133

Week 15: Help Me Handle My Bitterness (St. Luke 23:34)
- Day 1: God's Word For You Today: HATING YOU CAN KILL ME! 135
- Day 2: FORGIVENESS IS NOT FORGETTING WHAT HAPPENED! 137
- Day 3: IF YOU NEED IT YOU HAVE TO GIVE IT! 138
- Day 4: FORGIVENESS IS NOT FOR THEM IT'S FOR YOU! 139
- Day 5: THE SECRET TO DOING THIS IS…..YOU CAN'T, BUT GOD CAN! 140
- Day 6: HOLDING A GRUDGE IS HOLDING YOU HOSTAGE! 141
- Day 7: God's Word For You Today: LET IT GO! 142

Week 16: Help Me Handle It When What I Need Is An Upset (St. Matthew 28:9)
- Day 1: SOMETIMES THINGS GO FROM BAD TO WORST! 143
- Day 2: JUST BECAUSE IT LOOKS BAD DOESN'T MEAN IT WILL END THAT WAY! 145
- Day 3: LET YOUR ENEMIES DO THEIR PART! 147
- Day 4: DECLARE YOUR VICTORY FROM THE VERY BEGINNING! 149
- Day 5: YOU SHOULD BE OUT, BUT YOU'RE STILL IN! 151
- Day 6: HELL HAPPENS BUT REMEMBER HEAVEN DOES TOO! 153
- Day 7: YOUR SETBACK IS ONE THING, BUT YOUR UPSET IS ANOTHER! 155

ACKNOWLEDGEMENTS

Works like this one are never really the effort of just one person. Books that evolve over time are almost always the energy, effort, and endeavor of a community of people who help make them come to fruition. This book is a similitude of such. As a Pastor of a faithful congregation of believers, I have been graciously granted the privilege of sharing God's Word daily with other believers in the faith. In many instances, my sharing has come through sermons, Bible study lessons, special speaking engagements, and series studies, whereby I capture a category of study from the scriptures and squeeze it.

With this in mind, this book you now hold in your hand had its genesis during the global Pandemic of 2020. I did not know precisely what to teach, and one day, while in prayer, I felt compelled to teach believers via the World Wide Web just what the Bible said about perseverance and overcoming. Each week, I would reach into the hollowed pages of God's Word and look for passages, personalities, and paradigms where the Lord helped others persevere and overcome. The result was a thirty-five-week study that enlightened, empowered, and encouraged those who comprise the household of faith the world over.

In this stead, I must acknowledge the loving patience and perseverance of my wonderful wife, Lady Dorrie Adolph, whose prayers and kindness have been like a radiant light for me when life has been its darkest, and my amazing kids, Sumone and Jonathan, who stand by me and support my every endeavor. I forever appreciate the progressive mindset of my Executive Director, Minister Brooklyn Williams, who constantly says, "It's time to write again." I am forever indebted to my Executive Church Leaders, Dr. Karen Davis, Sister Felicia Young, and Rev. Jamison Malbrough, who are like cheerleaders with a Pompom shouting, "Go, Pastor, You Can Do It!"

I am humbled by Executive Church Leaders: Deacons, Trustees, Clergy, Coordinators, Directors, and Lay Leaders who share with me weekly and encourage my soul daily to keep teaching God's Word. I am blessed with the most incredible day staff in the world who help me share God's love with people from their desks daily: Pastor Albert Moore, Minister Kim Hardy, Sister Deeandria Darby, and Minister Linda Jones. I am so grateful for tenured Staff Leaders who have remained with me over the years to help me build the current Antioch: Jewel "Sue" Cooper, Lorraine Lemons, Pastor Jack Gay, Rev. Major M. Goldman III, and Rev. Alfred Beverly II for the graphic design of this book. And, to Dr. Porchanee White for editing this work so that it offers literary excellence to every reader that will peruse its pages.

Most importantly, I must thank God for the time, toil, and talent of a group of young people who emerged as the heroes of the Pandemic for the church and helped us to keep sharing the Gospel Message around the world virtually via the World Wide Web—hats off to my Media Ministry and Media Team.

INTRODUCTION

Dr. Cleopartrick Lady, retired professor of Sermon Preparation and Delivery at the Interdenominational Theological Center in Atlanta, Georgia, once made a statement in class that has remained with me since the day he made it. The remark was not included in his lecture. The statement was more like an off-the-cuff remark regarding Christian suffering that was so profound and prolific that it rested upon my heart like footprints in wet cement for the duration of my life as a believer in Jesus Christ. Here is what Dr. Lacy shared with his class as a sidebar note for young preachers who would dare preach the Gospel of our Lord. He said, "A Christian can't get to heaven with a manicure on their nails while Jesus has nail prints in His hands."

This statement shifted my view of human suffering like nothing else I had ever heard. God does not allow His children to be excluded from the crucible of pain, discomfort, disease, death, and conditions that arise from trauma and human tragedy. As a Senior Pastor of a young, growing church in the metropolis of Beaumont, Texas, I have had the awe-inspiring privilege of being near believers who have seen the worst of times and yet have remained faithful to the Lord Jesus Christ.

During the Pandemic, I watched as believers lost loved ones, struggled to make ends meet, pressed their way through financial woes, and somehow managed to keep on praying and growing in God's grace. Not to mention that numerous believers that I knew personally had perished from the hideous virus and even those that were diagnosed with it and could have also died, but the Lord just spared their lives and let them remain. Such occurrences pushed me to the scriptures to examine what the Bible teaches regarding how believers in Christ Jesus should persevere and overcome.

With this in mind, we find the raison d'etre of this work. This book is not a theological treatise on Christian doctrine, though it does contain doctrinal truth. This text is not a systematic study of the New or Old Testament, even though passages from both Testaments are used for analysis within the confines of this book. This work is a categorical look at what it means for God to help believers in Him handle what life throws at us and remain faithful.

In this stead, this book will journey through sixteen weeks of daily devotional study that will enlighten and empower you. On day 1 of each week, you will be introduced to our study passage that will be used for the next seven days, a parable, and a prayer. On Days 2-7, you will be encouraged to re-read the weekly study passage, consider a principle to practice in your daily walk with the Lord, read a parallel scripture verse related to our study for the week, and a prayer to whisper to God that comes from the lesson. It's all designed to help believers keep on, keeping on in the faith, knowing that if God is with us, He alone will help us handle it.

WEEK 1: Help Me Handle My New Start

Day 1

DO NOT EXPECT A REPEAT!

Our Passage of Study
Remember ye not the former things, Neither consider the things of old. Behold, I will do a new thing; Now it shall spring forth; shall ye not know it? I will even make a way in the wilderness, *And* rivers in the desert (Isaiah 43:18-19, KJV).

Today's Parable
Dr. Kempton Haynes led the Pastoral Care and Counseling Center in Atlanta, Georgia, in the early 1990's. I was a student of his while in seminary, and he led many group discussions with people in crisis mode every week. In short, if it wasn't drug addiction, it was mental instability, depression, and even demons of suicide. Initially, hearing some of the stories of these clients during our group sessions was shocking, to say the least. However, after a few months, they became almost routine.

One day, while gathering for a group session in the commons area, a clean-cut young man walked in that everyone knew and highly regarded. Dr. Haynes called the session to order, and this well-dressed, well-groomed guy began speaking first. He said, "Hi everybody, I'm Cleo, and I'm a no-good addict," to which the group replied in typical AA-like fashion, "Hi Cleo!" As Cleo talked with the group, his story was mind-blowing. He did not look like what he had been through. He had been through a divorce, the loss of his job, cancer of the stomach, addiction to alcohol, and addiction to both crack and heroin. Not to mention the fact that he was pronounced dead at Grady Memorial Hospital from what had appeared to be a drug overdose, but God spared his life!

Cleo told the group that he was in our counseling session because he wanted the Lord to help him with his start. He saw his being alive as a gift from God that marked a new beginning for him.

When Cleo finished sharing, Dr. Haynes looked at him and said, "Cleophus, God said, 'Don't expect a repeat! He will be doing some new things in your life, so get ready for it!'

As this book opens to the blessing of a brand new day, it marks the beginning of a new era in your life! I do not know what hardships have already found your address, what valleys you have endured, or what mistakes you have made in your personal past. I know this: God has left you alive this day with the benefit of a brand new start, and you should not expect a repeat!

WEEK 1: Help Me Handle My New Start

Receive this announcement in faith and take it to heart. God is about to do some new things in your life, so get ready for them!

Today's Prayer
Thank you, O Lord, for letting me live to see the bounty, blessing, and bliss of a season for the life you have given me. Forgive me for the mistakes of my past and the errors of my way. Now bless me, O Lord! Order my steps, help me select my friends, and guide my decisions like never before.

In The Name of Jesus, Amen.

WEEK 1: Help Me Handle My New Start

Day 2

GOD SAID, 'FORGET IT!'

Today's Passage
Remember ye not the former things, Neither consider the things of old. Behold, I will do a new thing; Now it shall spring forth; shall ye not know it? I will even make a way in the wilderness, *And* rivers in the desert (Isaiah 43:18-19, KJV).

Today's Point To Practice
The first six words of this passage should bless you like crazy. For the sake of redundancy, here they are again, "Remember ye, not the former things....." In short, God says, "I want you to forget it!" Here is a great devotional question worthy of pondering. Why would God instruct His people not to remember when He created human memory so that you would not forget? The reason for the command is that past triumphs and previous tragedies can hinder your future progress. If you spend too much time celebrating your high school diploma, you'll never earn your bachelor's degree. And, if you never get over the test you did not pass in high school, you'll never earn your diploma.

So hear this command from our creator and find healing, emancipation, and liberation in it, 'Forget it!"

Today's Push
Here is today's push: Do not let things behind you hinder, hamper, or harm what God has planned for you! What's ahead of you is what's best for you!

READ - Phil. 3:13-14

Today's Prayer
O God, my Father, please help me handle my mind and its memory. I tend to remember things I need to forget and forget things I need to remember. Help me forget anything that holds my future blessings hostage. And empower me to remember who you are, what you have said, and what you have done for me, knowing that you can do it again if you have done it before.

In The Name of Jesus, Amen.

WEEK 1: Help Me Handle My New Start

Day 3

NEW LOOKS GOOD ON YOU!

Today's Passage

Remember ye not the former things, Neither consider the things of old. Behold, I will do a new thing; Now it shall spring forth; shall ye not know it? I will even make a way in the wilderness, *And* rivers in the desert (Isaiah 43:18-19, KJV).

Today's Point To Practice

A new car drives smoother, a new pair of shoes stroll better, and a new outfit can make people say, "You look nice today!" Now imagine how a new future looks with God in control of it. Think of a tomorrow with God ordering your steps, guiding your thoughts, and opening new doors for you! If you are not shouting yet, you should be, and here is why: you have been graced with a brand new season of your life, and it is happening as you read this devotional note. God wants you to know that it will be filled with new things: new mercies every day, new blessings every moment, and a new, abundant life in Christ that is realized every minute of the day.

Wear your new because your new looks good on you!

READ - Lamentations 3:22-23

Today's Prayer

Jesus, today you have blessed me with a new day and a new lease on the life you have given me to live. Please know that my heart and my soul cry thank you! My asking of you right now is simply this: help me treasure what's new and use it in a way that is pleasing to you. I do not want to waste the grace you have extended to me, but I want to be found faithful with the newness of my life and my day.

In The Name of Jesus, Amen.

WEEK 1: Help Me Handle My New Start

Day 4

IT'S COMING!

Today's Passage
Remember ye not the former things, Neither consider the things of old. Behold, I will do a new thing; Now it shall spring forth; shall ye not know it? I will even make a way in the wilderness, *And* rivers in the desert (Isaiah 43:18-19, KJV).

Today's Point To Practice
There's nothing more exciting to watch than a child jumping up and down with excitement because a surprise they have been waiting for is now on the way. Not long ago, some kids stopped by the office. I asked if they had been good, and they said yes. I told them to hold on; I would be right back. I retreated to the back to grab one of my famous candy bags and could hear the excitement through the door. They were shouting, "It's coming! It's coming! It's Coming!"

When you read our weekly devotional passage, pay close attention to the words of guaranteed affirmation that Isaiah uses. "...I will...it shall...shall...I will..." It should give you the feeling of faith the children in my office had when I left to get my huge candy bag. When God says, "....I will...it shall....shall...I will..." rejoicing should follow because God cannot lie!

Here's the Word of the Lord for you today, and may you find hope, healing, and encouragement in them as you go through your day, "It's coming!"

READ - Deuteronomy 28

Today's Prayer
Merciful Master, I want you to know that I look forward in faith to every single solitary thing you have planned for the life you have given me! If you have commanded healing for me, it's coming. If you have commanded a blessing for me, it's coming. And if you have commanded strength for me amid my trials, I know it is coming. Thank you for being faithful to me, even when I am not always faithful.

And, Lord, give me the patience to wait for what's coming and rejoice like it's on the way because of your goodness and kindness. I know that what's coming from you in my life shall come to pass!

In The Name of Jesus, Amen.

WEEK 1: Help Me Handle My New Start

Day 5

YOUR GOD IS A WAY MAKER!

Today's Passage
Remember ye not the former things, Neither consider the things of old. Behold, I will do a new thing; Now it shall spring forth; shall ye not know it? I will even make a way in the wilderness, *And* rivers in the desert (Isaiah 43:18-19, KJV).

Today's Point To Practice
Notice the words of the text "I will even make a way…." The term used here in the passage comes from the Hebrew word *shim*, which means to arrange, install, or put something in place ahead of time. When you place this meaning back into the passage, it makes the blessing in the text explode with promise. You see, not only does God promise blessing that will come your way, but get this, He said, "I have made some arrangements, installed some things, and put some things in place to guarantee it.

In this stead, the Word of the Lord for you today is this: God is a way maker. What you need to make it has already been put in place. Your victory has already been set up for you to come out on top. The door you will walk through is already there and unlocked, ready for you to walk through. Now, here's the shout: the door that is obvious to you may look like a wall to everyone else. But when you know your God is a way maker, turn the knob, open the door, and let everybody know God made a way just for you!

READ-Isaiah 58:11

Today's Prayer
God, you are mighty, and you are strong! Today, I pause to celebrate your strength, power, and sovereign ability to do what no one else can. Thank you for being my way-maker and my way out of no way when things seem impossible. I have seen you do it time and time again. And right now, I want to thank you for how you will make things for me that I have not seen yet. Increase my faith to match the provisions coming in my direction, and I want to thank you for who you are in my life.

In The Name of Jesus, Amen.

WEEK 1: Help Me Handle My New Start

Day 6

EXPECT THE IMPOSSIBLE!

Today's Passage
Remember ye not the former things, Neither consider the things of old. Behold, I will do a new thing; Now it shall spring forth; shall ye not know it? I will even make a way in the wilderness, *And* rivers in the desert (Isaiah 43:18-19, KJV).

Today's Point To Practice
Not many of us know a lot about deserts. But here's one thing you can be confident about. They are dry and desolate places. In fact, the reason why the desert is called a desert is because it has no existing water supply. People can become dehydrated in the desert. Some people pass out and collapse due to the lack of water in the desert, and some even drop dead in the desert because they have no water at all. Now, imagine this: you will have to see some desert places in the days to come. You will not be exempt from them. But your God has arranged for you to have not just "a river" but "rivers" in the desert! It suggests that for every dry place, you will have access to a water supply to ensure your needs are met.

You might get hot, but you will not be thirsty!

Here's the point for today: in days to come, EXPECT THE IMPOSSIBLE!

READ-Psalms 1:1-3

Today's Prayer
God, I want you to know I will live the rest of my life expecting great things from you! I will not panic when I find myself in situations that are too hot for me to handle or too heated for me to deal with. Instead, I will thank you and bless you like crazy because your miraculous provisions will meet my needs. Thank you for being my provider and my miracle worker.

In The Name of Jesus, Amen.

WEEK 1: Help Me Handle My New Start

Day 7

THIS IS THE MOMENT YOU HAVE BEEN WAITING FOR!

Today's Passage
Remember ye not the former things, Neither consider the things of old. Behold, I will do a new thing; Now it shall spring forth; shall ye not know it? I will even make a way in the wilderness, *And* rivers in the desert (Isaiah 43:18-19, KJV).

Today's Point To Practice
Timing is everything! To be at the right place and time, doing the right thing can cause favor to fall in your lap. A crop harvested too soon will cause it to be too ripe. But, at the right time, that same harvest could yield a beautiful crop! Here's the point to practice and live from this moment forward: now is your appointed time! In fact, this is the moment you have been waiting for!

Your past mistakes have prepared you. Your lessons learned from the school of hard knocks have made you more resilient than ever before. Your encounters with God's mercy have made you trust Him more now than ever. And you are now in a place where you want more from the Lord than you ever have desired before in your life. This is the moment you have been waiting for!

Pray like it. Live like it. Walk like it. Plan like it. Work like it. Look like it. And trust God with it because the best is yet to come!

READ - Ecc. 3:11

Today's Prayer
Father, I do not know how much time I have left on the Earth. That is in your hands, and I trust you to do. Thank you for the time you have already given me. Each day has been a gift from you, and I am eternally grateful for them. Right now, I want to say thank you for this very moment. Today is the first day of the rest of my life, and this is the moment I have been waiting for. Use me for your glory, grow me in your grace, and bless me with your goodness, which is my sincere supplication and request.

In The Name of Jesus, Amen.

WEEK 2: Help Me Handle the Company I Keep

Day 1

GOD CHOOSES YOUR FAMILY BUT YOU PICK YOUR FRIENDS!

Our Passage of Study
Blessed is the man that walketh not in the counsel of the ungodly, nor standeth in the way of sinners, nor sitteth in the seat of the scornful (Psalms 1:1, KJV).

Today's Parable
The old cliches regarding human relationships are still true. You have heard many of them before—old sayings like, Birds of a feather flock together. If you lie with dogs, you will get up with fleas. If you run with wolves, you will learn how to howl. And, if you walk with thieves, they will teach you how to steal. In short, you are just like the company you keep.

Not long ago, I completed a job reference form for a young man applying for a very high-profile position with this huge software tech company from the West Coast. I enjoyed watching this young man grow up at the church, attend school, graduate from college, and get married. So when he asked me to serve as his reference, I considered it a great joy. Not to mention that the starting salary for the job he was applying for started at $285,000.00 a year plus other incentives.

He made it to the final round of the job interviews but was not selected. When I asked him why he was not chosen for the position, his answer blew me away. He informed me that the concluding interview involved three friends he had used as references on his application. This Fortune 500 company has a philosophy about relationships they use during the hiring process. The founder and CEO of the company says, "If you really want to see who you are hiring, sit and share with the interviewing candidates' best friends. When you meet them, it will tell you all that you need to know about the candidate you are looking to hire."

Here's some great questions to ponder. What does your immediate circle of friends say about you? If your friends were birds with feathers, would they be eagles, buzzards, vultures, chickens, hawks, or owls? What habits have you learned from your concentric circle of contact? Have you learned to pray, or have they taught you how to choose a hooka flavor, puff it, and shoot circles of smoke into the air?

Your choice of friends can bless you like crazy or curse you beyond your wildest dreams. The good news is the choice is yours because God chooses your family and lets you pick your friends!

WEEK 2: Help Me Handle the Company I Keep

Today's Prayer

Lord, I sincerely desire you to be my best friend. Anyone in my life who cannot walk with you cannot walk with me. With this in mind, O God, help me make the right decisions regarding the people I allow into my life. I want to be near people who love you, seek you, obey you, and follow you. Thank you for sending the right people into my life.

In The Name of Jesus, Amen.

WEEK 2: Help Me Handle the Company I Keep

Day 2

YOU SHOULD BLESS YOURSELF!

Today's Passage
Blessed is the man that walketh not in the counsel of the ungodly, nor standeth in the way of sinners, nor sitteth in the seat of the scornful (Psalms 1:1, KJV).

Today's Point To Practice
The book of Psalms is known as the heart of the Bible because it rests nearly in its center. It's the longest book in the scriptures, presenting one hundred and fifty Hebrew hymns. It concludes with these words, "…let everything that hath breath praise the Lord. Praise ye the Lord." In short, it ends with the people of God blessing God for His goodness. However, it commences with a purposeful way for you to bless yourself.

The word "*blessed*" in Psalms 1 comes from the Hebrew term *ashra*. It translates into English as the word happy. Thus, the longest book opens with a word that gives you the human right to make yourself happy. It gives you the right to bless yourself. A better verse translation should read like this, "Happy is the man…." What is it that makes the man happy? He will soon make choices regarding the people he will allow to be in his company.

Today's Push
Here is today's push: Don't stress yourself; bless yourself. Look at your life as a valuable commodity worth dying to save, and treat it not like trash that's worthless. Handle it like a treasure loaded with innumerable, incalculable blessings waiting to come forth.

READ - Proverbs 22:24-25

Today's Prayer
Lord of Heaven and God of the Earth, help me choose the right people for my life. Forgive me for making some really poor choices in the past. Thank you for the blessed privilege of making new decisions starting today.

In The Name of Jesus, Amen.

WEEK 2: Help Me Handle the Company I Keep

Day 3

RUN FROM BAD ADVICE!

Today's Passage
Blessed is the man that walketh not in the counsel of the ungodly, nor standeth in the way of sinners, nor sitteth in the seat of the scornful (Psalms 1:1, KJV).

Today's Point To Practice
This one verse gives you three groups of people that you should avoid. The first group that Christians should run from are those defined as the "…counsel of the ungodly…" The term *counsel* refers to those we gain advice from and those we seek direction from. The word *ungodly* relates to those people who reject God. They are people who simply say you don't need God; you can do what you desire to do without Him. Be careful because some ungodly people are nice, successful folks who appear to have done well for themselves. When they speak to you, they boast about their good decisions, hard work, and business acumen. They never brag or boast about God. In their minds, God is nonexistent when it comes to the things they have accomplished.

Remember this: Any advice that erases our need for God is bad advice from the start! Here's today's lesson: Run from bad advice.

READ - 1 Kings 12:8-12, KJV

Today's Prayer
Jesus, there are times I admire certain people's achievements. It bothers me when I do not hear them mention or acknowledge you. Today, I have discovered these people are what the Bible calls the "ungodly." Lord, order my steps and direct my paths to people who love telling others what you have done for them.

In The Name of Jesus, Amen.

WEEK 2: Help Me Handle the Company I Keep

Day 4

STAND FOR SOMETHING OR FALL FOR ANYTHING!

Today's Passage
Blessed is the man that walketh not in the counsel of the ungodly, nor standeth in the way of sinners, nor sitteth in the seat of the scornful (Psalms 1:1, KJV).

Today's Point To Practice
Okay, so let's be clear: everyone sins. In fact, the Bible says, "All have sinned and come short of the glory of God" (Romans 3:23, KJV). However, in Psalms 1 we are told to avoid "....standing in the way of sinners…" The word used to describe "*sinners*" is a term that refers to those persons who sin without remorse or repentance and enjoy it. It suggests that these people know what they are doing is wrong, have no regrets about the wrong, enjoy the wrong, and celebrate their wrongdoings with others who do wrong like they do.

The danger of being near a *sinner* like this is found in the fact that they know right from wrong and choose wrong without ever asking God to forgive them.

When in the company of sinners who do wrong, willingly take a stand for God and do good! And remember this: if you don't stand for something, you will fall for anything!

READ - 2 Cor. 6:17

Today's Prayer
Eternal God, my Father, I approach you right now with a spirit of gratitude. I'm thankful because I have been near people who sinned openly and enjoyed every moment with them. Yet, you have brought me close enough to you right now to know better and to want to do better. Lord, I want you to give me the strength to stand for you even when it is unpopular. Forgive me for my previous failures, and thank you, Jesus, for the blessing of another chance.

In The Name of Jesus, Amen.

WEEK 2: Help Me Handle the Company I Keep

Day 5

BAD COMPANY CORRUPTS GOOD MANNERS!

Today's Passage
Blessed is the man that walketh not in the counsel of the ungodly, nor standeth in the way of sinners, nor sitteth in the seat of the scornful (Psalms 1:1, KJV).

Today's Point To Practice
If you put a rotten apple in a barrel with freshly picked apples, the rotten apple will corrupt the good apples and make them bad. Believe it or not, the influence of bad people is just as powerful as that of a bad apple. The Psalmist warns us not to "... sit in the seat of the scornful." The scornful are those who not only do what is wrong in the sight of the Lord and enjoy it but get others to join them in doing what the Lord says, not to do without remorse. A person like this should be considered dangerous and avoided at all costs. They speak evil of the things of God and rejoice when others join their slander.

There is an old saying that holds true: " Bad company corrupts good manners." Here's the point to practice today: if you are near people influencing your life to move in the wrong direction, don't keep them near you; cut them off and move forward.

READ-1 Cor. 15:33

Today's Prayer
Lord, give me the strength to break relational ties with anyone in my life who is not helping me walk in the same direction you are walking in. Help me discern the motives, intentions, and spirits of the people in my life. Guide me in my decision-making, and know I will follow where you lead. Thank you, Jesus, for who you are and what you mean to me.

In The Name of Jesus, Amen.

WEEK 2: Help Me Handle the Company I Keep

Day 6

WITH THE WRONG PEOPLE IN YOUR LIFE, THINGS CAN GO FROM BAD TO WORSE!

Today's Passage
Blessed is the man that walketh not in the counsel of the ungodly, nor standeth in the way of sinners, nor sitteth in the seat of the scornful (Psalms 1:1, KJV).

Today's Point To Practice
Take a moment and closely observe what you see in our passage listed above. Did you notice the downward spiral? Check this out: we are warned not to "walk" in the counsel of the ungodly. We are then encouraged not to "stand" in the way of sinners. Finally, we are told not to "sit" in the seat of the scornful. The downward progression is that we go from walking to standing and from standing to sitting. In a practical sense, with the wrong people in your life, it is possible to go from progress (walking) to making no progress (standing) and from making no progress to actually living in a mode where you regress (sitting).

Here's the bottom line: Things can go from bad to worse with the wrong people in your life.

READ- Psalms 37:1-4

Today's Prayer
Lord Jesus, I want the right people in my life. I do not wish to be affiliated with anyone you did not send or authorize. Please show me the way and light my path in my relationships. I love you, Lord, and thank you,

In The Name of Jesus, Amen.

WEEK 2: Help Me Handle the Company I Keep

Day 7

SOME PEOPLE YOU CUT AND OTHERS YOU KEEP!

Today's Passage
Blessed is the man that walketh not in the counsel of the ungodly, nor standeth in the way of sinners, nor sitteth in the seat of the scornful (Psalms 1:1, KJV).

Today's Point To Practice
Okay, so here's today's point to practice: at what point do you cut them, and at what point do you keep them? The answer to these questions rests purely in the study passage from this week. Whenever a person in your space regularly influences you to go backward in your walk with God, you should cut them. When a person helps you rekindle sins you have been delivered from in the past, cut them. And, if you are near people who take joy in watching you live in sin and call the sin you are in a good time, cut them and move on!

Keep those persons in your life who are positive, helpful, prayerful, spiritual, and meaningful and who will celebrate your progress and success when your life is being blessed by the Lord and headed in the right direction! You want to see your life in Christ go onward and upward, not backward and downward.

READ - Proverbs 13:20

Today's Prayer
Lord, thank you for the positive, loving, caring, wondering, and meaningful people in my life. I consider them ambassadors you sent to help me along the way. Forgive me for allowing the wrong people into my life, and I celebrate you giving me the courage to release people who do not mean me well so I can move progressively onward. Soli Deo Gloria!

In The Name of Jesus, Amen.

WEEK 3: Help Me Handle This Bank Account of Mine

Day 1

YOU ARE NOT SUPPOSED TO BE BROKE!

Our Passage of Study
And she went and did according to the saying of Elijah: and she, and he, and her house, did eat many days.

And the barrel of meal wasted not, neither did the cruse of oil fail, according to the word of the LORD, which he spake by Elijah. (1 Kings 17:15-16, KJV).

Today's Parable
Prayer requests. They are something that I take joy in responding to because I believe in the power, potency, and practice of prayer. In short, I believe the Lord of Heaven hears and responds to our prayers from Earth. One day, while looking through a litany of prayer requests, one stood out like a crimson cord running through a beautiful white quilt. It read, "Pastor Adolph, I need help, and it's urgent. I work every day, and I'm still broke. No one knows it because I look like I have it all together, but I cannot pay my light bill, my car note is a struggle, and my house note is behind. I have a decent job and a part-time hustle selling Mary K. I can't talk to anyone about what I'm going through. I'm broke, and I work every day. I feel like the devil has cursed me in the area of my money, and I need God. Please ask the Lord to help me!"

I took a moment to re-read this request, which leaped out at me, and I started praying immediately. She said, "I'm broke and work every day." This stood out to me because I have had a season of my life where I worked my regular job, a part-time job, and a full-time hustle and did not have any money in the bank. I could relate to this part of the prayer request. Here's a great devotional question for you to ponder: have you ever worked every day, and all you had to show for it was clothes, cars, shoes, and bills with your name on them?

The heart of this lesson is to look at God's plan for your finances and make money moves that will bless you like crazy in the future. If you are financially solvent, this lesson will be a reminder of sorts. However, if you are going through a season of financial struggle and your prayer request sounds like the one listed above, this lesson will feel like somebody just gave you a bottle of cold water on a hot Texas summer day in 105-degree heat. In short, it is going to bless you.

God has something to say about what is in your bank account, and when you apply His principles to the resources He has entrusted you with, blessing, favor, and increase are always

WEEK 3: Help Me Handle This Bank Account of Mine

the results. This week's study passage will be 1 Kings 17. We will highlight verses 15-16 of the passage, but we will occasionally study pieces and portions of it all.

Help is on the way for your bank account, and the answer to many of your monetary concerns is now in your hands!

Today's Prayer
Lord Jesus, thank you for blessing me by increasing what's in my bank account. Yet, God, I have come to you right now because I struggle from time to time financially, and I work every day. There are times that it feels like everything breaks at the same time, and my financial portrait looks terrible. Sometimes, I can see the light at the end of the tunnel, but I realize there is no light, and I'm stuck there. Help me, O God, possess the financial wealth you have assigned to my hands. Give me the faith to make the necessary changes and the endurance to press my way into the financial blessing that would set me for the rest of my life.

In The Name of Jesus, Amen.

WEEK 3: Help Me Handle This Bank Account of Mine

Day 2

God's Word For You Today: GOD WILL PROVIDE!

Today's Passage
And she went and did according to the saying of Elijah: and she, and he, and her house, did eat many days.
And the barrel of meal wasted not, neither did the cruse of oil fail, according to the word of the LORD, which he spake by Elijah. (1 Kings 17:15-16, KJV).

Today's Point To Practice
Take a moment and read 1 Kings 17:1-16 right quick. It should only take about ninety seconds. And, while you read, note the things God provides. This story is amazing. God sends Elijah to Zarapheth during a famine to find a widow. She's poor and has just enough resources to eat, feed her child, and die. She is not lazy. In fact, when Elijah spots her she is picking up sticks. In short, she's industrious. However, what she is about to discover is the one point I want you to practice, recall, remember, and live by for the rest of your life, and it is this: God will provide.

This Biblical truth will change your life forever once you internalize it by faith. Often, we feel like the Lord is not going to provide. However, the irony is that we do this with His provisions staring us in the face. Consequently, the real issue confronting us is that we fall into demonic tricks and traps when we take God's provisions, steward them poorly, and end up in poverty.

As you read the story, what did you notice that God provided? Here's the point of today's lesson: God provided! Please hold on to this emphatic Biblical truth if you remember nothing else about today's lesson. God will provide!

READ - Exodus 17:6

Today's Prayer
God, you have always been a way-maker, a provider, and a bill-payer for me. Thank you for never leaving me in the condition you found me in. Lord, my prayer today is that you would please show yourself mighty and strong by providing for me again. However, I want you to move me from being broke to sound financially. I know that you can; I only ask that you would.

In The Name of Jesus, Amen.

WEEK 3: Help Me Handle This Bank Account of Mine

Day 3

LITTLE BECOMES MUCH WHEN USED THE RIGHT WAY!

Today's Passage
And she went and did according to the saying of Elijah: and she, and he, and her house, did eat many days. And the barrel of meal wasted not, neither did the cruse of oil fail, according to the word of the LORD, which he spake by Elijah. (1 Kings 17:15-16, KJV).

Today's Point To Practice
When managing the resources in your account, remember this: it is not what you have. It is how you use what God has given you. In this week's lesson story, God sends Elijah to a brook and feeds him twice daily. He has food and water because God is taking care of him. His brook runs dry, and the Lord moves him upward and onward to the city of Zarapheth during a famine. To make matters worse, he assigns Elijah to a poor widow with very little. The shout of today's lesson is that little in the right hands can become much when used the right way.

The widow says, "All I have is a little meal and a tiny bit of oil in my cruse…" Notice this: even though she does not have much, she will use it wisely and not wastefully.

Our prevailing problem often rests right here. We are often wasteful and lack wisdom when it comes to handling money. We buy what we like and don't need and then have no money left for things we need to pay for and cannot live safely without. In short, we will buy a designer handbag and struggle to pay the light bill. We will use one hundred dollars a week at Starbucks when you can make our coffee, spend $15.00, and have enough coffee for a month. It is how we use what we have.

Here's today's point to practice. Look carefully at your finances, eliminate wasteful spending, and prepare to see an increase right away! READ - St. John 6:1-14, KJV

Today's Prayer
Lord Jesus, help me reorganize my spending priorities. Give me the faith and obedience, to begin with, including you with my tithe, and look carefully at all of my other expenses that are primary first. Forgive me for the impulsive, needless spending I sometimes feel guilty of. Thank you for this moment when the changes that I am going to make will result in a harvest that is coming my way.

In The Name of Jesus, Amen.

WEEK 3: Help Me Handle This Bank Account of Mine

Day 4

OBEDIENCE AND OVERFLOW ARE ALWAYS EQUALS!

Today's Passage
And she went and did according to the saying of Elijah: and she, and he, and her house, did eat many days. And the barrel of meal wasted not, neither did the cruse of oil fail, according to the word of the LORD, which he spake by Elijah. (1 Kings 17:15-16, KJV).

Today's Point To Practice
It is known as modern-day profanity. Kids hate it, adults despise it, and parishioners in church frown on it every time it is used. What is it you ask? It is the term obey. We hate being obedient. This term is hated in our culture because it goes against what people practice daily. In the current culture, people of every age group do what they want to do when they want to do it. So, to hear someone tell you that you must obey is typically followed by disobedience and utter rebellion. However, remember this: if you want to see your poverty transformed to become plenty, if you're going to see your lack become more than enough, and watch your bank account go from a negative balance to a positive one, you must find it in your heart to obey!

Look carefully at the first words of this week's study passage. It reads like this, "And she went and did according to the saying of Elijah…" In short, she did what the Lord told her to do. More specifically, God spoke to Elijah, and Elijah talked to her. She did what God said to do, prosperity found her, and her lack disappeared.

Hear this: When the man of God says tithe, be obedient and tithe. When the man of God says stop wasteful spending, cut wasteful spending, and prepare to start saving. The system works, and when God is obeyed, the blessings just start to flow. READ - 1 Samuel 15:22

Today's Prayer
God, I want you to have mercy on me and forgive me. There have been times, moments, and even seasons where I have not been a good steward of the resources you have placed in my hand. The result has been that I work hard every day but have little to show for it. As of right now, I am starting over. The tithe is yours, and I will give it to you. I will, by faith, reprioritize and reorganize my life so that my needs and wants are never mixed up again. Give me the strength and perseverance not just to talk the talk but also faith to walk the walk. Thank you, Jesus, for the increase that will find me due to my obedience as it relates to my finances.

In The Name of Jesus, Amen.

WEEK 3: Help Me Handle This Bank Account of Mine

Day 5

WHAT YOU HAVE NOW IS NOT ALL GOD WANTS YOU TO POSSESS!

Today's Passage
And she went and did according to the saying of Elijah: and she, and he, and her house, did eat many days.
And the barrel of meal wasted not, neither did the cruse of oil fail, according to the word of the LORD, which he spake by Elijah. (1 Kings 17:15-16, KJV).

Today's Point To Practice
God's Word For You Today recorded should cause your heart and soul to rejoice! Read it again. Can you hear the vocal cords of God's voice wrapped around this statement for you? The blessings of our Lord that are headed your direction are not slack concerning His provisions for your life.

Look just for a moment at verse 15. Pay close attention to the second half of the verse. It reads like this, "…..and she, and he, and her house, did eat many days." Wait, how do you go from making a small cake, eating it and wanting to die, to you and your entire house grubbing for many days? It happens when you realize by faith and receive by action that God has more in store for you than you could ever imagine!

Wait, here's the shout: When you are faithful with what is in your account, God is not just going to bless you; He is about to use your life as a vehicle and vessel to bless your entire family!

Here's your point to practice for the week: when you organize your finances the right way, it will come with benefits attached, not just for you but for your children's college fund, your retirement fund, and blessings for your family because WHAT YOU HAVE NOW IS NOT ALL GOD WANTS YOU TO HAVE!

READ - Deuteronomy 8:18

Today's Prayer
Eternal God, our Father, please use my life to bless not just me but also my entire family through me.

In The Name of Jesus, Amen.

WEEK 3: Help Me Handle This Bank Account of Mine

Day 6

God's Word For You Today: THE FLOOD GATES ARE NOW OPEN!

Today's Passage
And she went and did according to the saying of Elijah: and she, and he, and her house, did eat many days.
And the barrel of meal wasted not, neither did the cruse of oil fail, according to the word of the LORD, which he spake by Elijah. (1 Kings 17:15-16, KJV).

Today's Point To Practice
When appropriately managed, money has four realms of blessing attached to it. First of all, you work hard to earn it. With proper management and God's favor comes the second level of money management, which takes place when you get others to help you gain the money you are making. A good example is when Peter had to get his friends to help him with the fish he had caught (Luke 5:5-6). Peter had to hire help just to get the job done. The third dimension of money growth is when your money now works for you. With solid investments, your money makes money while you do other things. The last realm of money management occurs when you have enough wealth to live on, and the money you have worked to earn empowers the next generation.

When this story ends, the shout of the day is seen when these words are recorded, "And the barrel of meal wasted not, neither did the cruse of oil fail...." A better way to say the same thing would be to say, "The floodgates are now open!" The widow in this story has gone from barely making it to feeding everyone in her house with food to spare. In short, she never saw shortage, lack, or poverty again.

How would you act if God blessed you so much that it ended poverty for your family on Earth? This is God's plan, and it starts with you, so get with the program!

And remember this: the floodgates are now open!

READ - Joshua 24:13-15

Today's Prayer
May the floodgates of the blessing of the Lord find my life and flood my family.

In The Name of Jesus, Amen.

WEEK 3: Help Me Handle This Bank Account of Mine

Day 7

God's Word For You Today: THE CHOICE IS YOURS!

Today's Passage
And she went and did according to the saying of Elijah: and she, and he, and her house, did eat many days.
And the barrel of meal wasted not, neither did the cruse of oil fail, according to the word of the LORD, which he spake by Elijah. (1 Kings 17:15-16, KJV).

Today's Point To Practice
Do you remember the young lady I told you about on day one who urgently requested prayer from me? Here's what I told her, and it's the same thing that I share with you. God's plan for your financial future is not poverty. Being poor does not make you godly; it just makes you poor. If you really want God to change your financial outlook, it can happen and start today, but the choice is yours.

You have to decide whether you are going to shop or save. You have to determine whether you will wear name brands that look great or be proud of your name and put some money aside to grow your finances. You have to decide whether you will eat out every day or learn how to cook for less than half the price and save hundreds of dollars every month. You have to decide to use the money and resources that the Lord gives you in a godly way so that when all is settled, you see the blessing of the Lord in every facet of your life including, but not limited to, your finances.

Your financial future is literally resting in your next choices! If you are sick of being broke and working every day, shift your thinking from wants to needs and necessities!

And remember, the choice is yours!

READ -Joshua 24:15

Today's Prayer
Lord, I realize that my past money choices have not always been the best. I humbly ask you to give me the wherewithal to make better financial decisions with the money you have blessed me with so that my financial outlook will have your favor and blessing written all over it.

In The Name of Jesus, Amen.

WEEK 4: Help Me Handle How I Feel

Day 1

YOUR DUE SEASON IS NOW DUE!

Our Passage of Study
And let us not be weary in well doing for in due season we shall reap if you faint not. As we have therefore opportunity, let us do good unto all men, especially unto them who are of the household of faith (Galatians 6:9 KJV).

Today's Parable
Amid the soulful 70s came music from Detroit, Michigan, that rocked the nation and marked an entire generation. People who can remember music from this era have a right to call themselves "old school." Barry Gordy and the Motown sound will live forever. One of the many famed artists from that time in American history was a man named Marvin Gaye. While the war in Vietnam was raging and racism in the United States was flaming, Marvin said, "...it makes me wanna holla and throw up both of my hands!"

It was his way of saying, "Help me handle how I feel." During that era, human emotions, including irritation, agitation, and frustration, often overwhelmed people. Racism, classism, sexism, and the threat of the spread of communism caused riots, public uprisings, and social demonstrations as people struggled with how they felt about what was going on.

Here's the absolute truth of today's story: people are struggling similarly today. One look at life and what it can bring your way is enough to make you look toward heaven and say, "Lord, help me handle how I feel!" In fact, take a look at your own life for a moment. Be honest. Have you ever felt like giving up? Quitting? Have you ever felt like throwing in the towel? If you answered yes, you know what it feels like to "...wanna holla and throw up both of your hands."

What do you do when life puts you in such a predicament? Wait before you respond; we will spend the week looking at Galatians 6:9 for the right answer.

In the meantime, let's do something that Christians and believers should do when life makes them want to quit: let's pray.

Today's Prayer
Lord of heaven, there are times when I must admit that life gets the best of me. There are times when I feel angry, depressed, dejected, disgusted, and sometimes I even feel depleted to the point that I just want to give up. However, I know I do not sew and reap in the same season. God help

WEEK 4: Help Me Handle How I Feel

me hold on. Give me the strength not to quit. And, if I'm too weak to hold on, let me have more of your strength so that I will not let go.

Thank you, Lord, because your strength in me never gets weak, never wanes, and always works.

In The Name of Jesus, Amen.

WEEK 4: Help Me Handle How I Feel

Day 2

DON'T QUIT!

Today's Passage
And let us not be weary in well doing: for in due season we shall reap, if we faint not. As we have therefore opportunity, let us do good unto all *men*, especially unto them who are of the household of faith (Gal. 6:9, KJV).

Today's Point To Practice
Have you ever felt like throwing up both hands and just walking away and giving up? It can happen to the best of us. When Paul writes this Epistle to the Galatians, he uses the term *enkakeo* to describe what it feels like to get really exhausted. *En* means to be without and *kakeo* translates the desire to keep going or to lose heart. When you put these two word portions together the word weary (*enkakeo*) means to lose the desire to keep going. It means to become discouraged.

Here's a personal devotional question for you to ponder. Have you ever reached a point where quitting made more sense than continuing? Have you ever been there when you just wanted to walk off and say, "Forget it"? If you have, it is then that these words should come to life in your journey because the only way for you to lose is to quit too soon.

Today's Push
Here is today's push: No matter what conditions life throws your way and no matter how you may feel about it, never quit! Never give up! Never give in! Never let it get the best of you! Do not throw your hands up and walk away. Your faith in God shouts, "Throw your hands up in worship and press on!" You can make it with God on your side. He will not fail you!

Today's Prayer
O Lord my God, there have been times when I have wanted to give up, walk off, quit, and drop everything. Give me your strength today to keep on keeping on when feelings like this seek to hinder me.

In The Name of Jesus, Amen.

WEEK 4: Help Me Handle How I Feel

Day 3

YOU'RE NOT ALONE!

Today's Passage

And let us not be weary in well doing: for in due season we shall reap if we faint not. As we have therefore opportunity, let us do good unto all *men*, especially unto them who are of the household of faith (Gal. 6:9, KJV).

Today's Point To Practice

One of the greatest tricks of the enemy is to make you feel like you are all alone. The devil is great at making you feel like no one else in the world understands or really cares. When this happens to you, and it will if you really love the Lord, remember, the devil is a liar! God cares, and you are never alone!

Look at today's passage again and notice the plural verbs used in the text. The word "us" appears twice, the term "we" is mentioned three times, and "them" is mentioned once. Here's the point: all these words refer to more than one person, suggesting that you are not by yourself. There are others in the household of faith who understand your plight, have endured your pain, and have decided to keep pressing on. If they can make it, you can too.

And never forget this: no matter how alone you may feel, you're alone with good company because God is on your side! Here's some great news: you are not alone!

READ-St. Matthew 28:20

Today's Prayer

Lord Jesus, there are times when I feel alone and lonely, and sometimes, even a feeling of being abandoned rises in my mind. Master, in times like these, help me remember and never forget that this is a lie from the pit of hell because you are always with me. Thank you, Jesus, for being my Shepherd who never leaves me alone.

In The Name of Jesus, Amen.

WEEK 4: Help Me Handle How I Feel

Day 4

THERE'S A REASON FOR YOUR SEASON!

Today's Passage
And let us not be weary in well doing: for in due season we shall reap if we faint not. As we have therefore opportunity, let us do good unto all *men*, especially unto them who are of the household of faith (Gal. 6:9, KJV).

Today's Point To Practice
The worst thing for a farmer to do is give up on his harvest before his crop comes in. You see, here's the point: You do not sow and reap in the same season. If you are going to have a wonderful harvest, you have to go through the process if you want to see the product. A farmer has to till the ground, sow the seeds, water what's planted, wait with the patience of a job, and then endure until his season for plucking what has been planted grows.

The same is true for you. God has a reason for every season in your life, so learn how to be thankful no matter what season you may find yourself in.

If you are in a season of struggle, be thankful. God is producing the strength you will need for the future. If you are in a season of losses, be thankful. God is showing you that He alone is your most significant gain. If you are in a season of learning, be thankful. God is increasing your wisdom because He has plans to prosper you. If you are in a season of defeat, be grateful. God is preparing you for a comeback from your setback that will bless you. And if you are in a season of prosperity, be thankful. The favor of God rests upon you, and His fruitfulness is your divine supply.

READ-1 Thessalonians 5:17

Today's Prayer
Eternal God, my Father, I thank you for the seasons of my life thus far because with each season have come lessons that have changed my life for the better. Use the season I'm in for your glory and my good.

In The Name of Jesus,
Amen

WEEK 4: Help Me Handle How I Feel

Day 5

DON'T LET BEING TIRED TAKE YOU OUT!

Today's Passage
And let us not be weary in well doing: for in due season we shall reap if we faint not. As we have therefore opportunity, let us do good unto all *men*, especially unto them who are of the household of faith (Gal. 6:9, KJV).

Today's Point To Practice
It is human to become tired. But never let being tired take you out. The blessing of reaping is only for those who "…faint not." In other words, everyone will want a portion of your harvest when it comes in, but not everyone has endured, persevered, and pressed their way as you have.

The word *faint* Paul uses is a medical term for someone who passes out while traveling in extremely hot conditions. In many instances, it refers to someone who has become dehydrated and cannot continue.

Did you know that both dehydration and overheating can be treated by simply making two minor adjustments? Rest is the remedy for fainting. And water is the fix for dehydration. Rest and water. Doesn't this ring a bell for you? If it does not, it should. In Psalm 23, we are told that we have a shepherd who provides both if we stay connected to Him.

READ-Psalms 23

Today's Prayer
Lord Jesus, I want to be honest with you right now. There are times I get tired, and I feel like being tired is taking me out. I have even had moments where I was running on fumes, and I knew it, though others could not tell. Please, Lord, refill, refuel, and restore me with your strength, your spirit, your joy, and your love.

In The Name of Jesus, Amen.

WEEK 4: Help Me Handle How I Feel

Day 6

KEEP DOING THE RIGHT THING!

Today's Passage
And let us not be weary in well doing: for in due season we shall reap, if we faint not. As we have therefore opportunity, let us do good unto all *men*, especially unto them who are of the household of faith (Gal. 6:9, KJV).

Today's Point To Practice
It can be frustrating for the believer in Christ when people who do wrong prosper while they do right and struggle. Have you ever been there? Where your clubbing, pubbing, sipping, lying, no good co-worker has blessings falling in their lap, and you have doors slammed in your face right after you have fasted and prayed. Moments like this can be very disheartening. It can be rough when you watch people who do not pray or care to go to church receive healing in their bodies while you are in the house of worship every single time the doors open, and yet your illness and infirmities continue.

As Paul writes to the churches of Galatia, he emphasizes your continued doing "…..good towards all men, especially unto them who are of the household of faith." In short, do not stop doing the right thing! Keep on praying, keep on serving, keep on helping, keep on pushing, keep on running for the Lord, and keep on doing what is right in the eyes of the Lord.

Here's the point for today: keep doing the right thing!

READ-Philippians 3:12-14

Today's Prayer
There are times, O Lord when I question why you bless those who do wrong and allow suffering to those who are trying to do right. Forgive me for getting out of my lane and questioning you. I repent and it will not happen again. I have decided to trust you more than ever before. With this in mind, I ask one favor of you this morning: Lord, help me do the right thing no matter what.

In The Name of Jesus, Amen.

WEEK 4: Help Me Handle How I Feel

Day 7

IT'S MY CHOICE!

Today's Passage
And let us not be weary in well doing: for in due season we shall reap, if we faint not. As we have therefore opportunity, let us do good unto all *men*, especially unto them who are of the household of faith (Gal. 6:9, KJV).

Today's Point To Practice
In the soulful 1970s, Marvin Gaye told the whole world how he was feeling. He said, "It makes me want to holla and throw up both of my hands." However, here's something very powerful, poignant, and precious for you to never forget. You are the decision maker on how you feel. No matter what happens to you, no matter what comes your way, no matter what blessing or burden finds your life, how you think about what is going on is your decision.

Your decisions are so powerful that even God Himself does not seek to make decisions for you. Think about that for a moment. We believe in a God that spoke galaxies into existence, yet this same God will not make up your mind for you. This is so powerful that it should make you rejoice right now! Here's today's key point to practice: THE CHOICE IS YOURS! If you feel like a conqueror, the choice is yours. If you feel defeated, the choice is yours. If you feel like you can move a mountain, the choice is yours. If you feel overwhelmed, the choice is yours. And, if you feel like it's going to be alright, the choice is yours.

Never forget this: the way you handle how you feel is to remember that your feelings are under your command, and the choice is yours!

READ-Joshua 24

Today's Prayer
Lord, I thank you today for being who you are and blessing me the way you have. God, thank you for the volitional right to choose. I prefer to be happy, trust you, pray, worship, serve, fight forward, and choose Jesus Christ! Thank you for the power of choice.

In The Name of Jesus, Amen.

WEEK 5: Help Me Handle It When There's Somebody for Everybody but Me!

Day 1

DIFFERENT LEVELS CAN EXPOSE NEW DEVILS!

Our Passage of Study
Be ye not unequally yoked together with unbelievers: for what fellowship hath righteousness with unrighteousness? And what communion hath light with darkness? (2 Cor. 6:14, KJV)

Today's Parable
The only way the devil can destroy you is through an attack that comes from close proximity. The enemy typically uses people we can trust to do his dirty work. With this in mind, when you meet new people who somehow end up in your immediate space and your face, you should ask yourself this one question: "Who sent them?"

Single saints who desire marriage should be careful in this area. After all, how can you meet a desired mate if you throw everyone away that comes your way if you feel that they may not have it all together? Here's a tell-tale sign that is sure to come to pass. Be most watchful of demonic attacks when you start to feel like there's somebody for everybody but you!

A dear friend of mine has a 24-year-old daughter who just finished nursing school and is now a Registered Nurse. While in nursing school, she could not afford to go on a date with a decent guy. She told her mother she was sick of attending weddings and being a bridesmaid. She wanted to be a bride. She went to a party one evening and met a friend of a friend who openly admitted that he was a Christian but did not take the whole "religious thing" too seriously. He was charming, handsome, and so nice to her. They started to date, and she discovered that he was abusive, controlling, manipulative, vengeful, and a big-time user. Before long, she found herself bound to him and not to God! It was then she discovered that different levels can expose new devils.

Being unequally yoked with unbelievers is serious business if you are single and seeking God for a spouse. Be watchful when God opens new doors for you and causes an increase in finding you. That's when the enemy increases his attacks against you.

Today's Prayer
God, I pray for supernatural wisdom and guidance for every believer who desires to be married. Expose the enemy, dismiss demons, and push back the devil's attacks so those you send our way can reach us because they are people with a purpose connected with our faith and fate in you.

In The Name of Jesus, Amen.

WEEK 5: Help Me Handle It When There's Somebody for Everybody but Me!

Day 2

DON'T IGNORE THE WARNING SIGNS!

Today's Passage

Be ye not unequally yoked together with unbelievers: for what fellowship hath righteousness with unrighteousness? And what communion hath light with darkness? (2 Cor. 6:14, KJV)

Today's Point To Practice

She lies compulsively. He never seems to go to church. She has a shaky background. He drinks daily. She complains about everything. He has a bad temper. She is messy and finds the time to be in everybody's business. He spends a lot of time playing video games. She shops all of the time and always needs money to pay her light bill. He is sneaky. She is flirty and calls it being friendly. He is very friendly and loves to greet ladies with a hug and sometimes, even a kiss on the cheek, and is always hugging people. She has four kids, and they have four different fathers. He has a shoe box filled with strange-looking herbs and says they are for medicinal use only. She guards her phone like it is connected to the gold in Fort Knox. He is always tipping away to take "business" calls in private. She has five different personalities, none of which are similar. He is down in the dumps until ESPN comes on. She goes to church but never prays or reads her Bible. He prays, but his God is a statue glued to the dashboard of his car.

Warning signs! Do not miss them. God is a God of revelation and sends you warning signs that you should pay attention to. If you miss the signs, you will miss your exit, get dropped at an unfamiliar location, and end up lost in a place you cannot get out of, connected to people you cannot escape.

Today's Push

When people show you who they are, do not try to change them! Believe them and leave them where you found them. In short, when God shows you clear-cut warning signs, run! You can do bad all bad yourself. Run! You'd rather be alone than be connected to anyone who will pull you downwards, take you backward, and hinder you from going in the right direction forward.
READ - Psalms 1:1

Today's Prayer

Lord, bless me with a spirit of discernment regarding those nearest me and whom I may be interested in.

In Jesus Name, Amen.

WEEK 5: Help Me Handle It When There's Somebody for Everybody but Me!

Day 3

ASK THEM THIS QUESTION: WHAT DO YOU REALLY BELIEVE?

Today's Passage
Be ye not unequally yoked together with unbelievers: for what fellowship hath righteousness with unrighteousness? And what communion hath light with darkness? (2 Cor. 6:14, KJV)

Today's Point To Practice
One of the things that should be the cornerstone and capstone of every Christian relationship is what we share as it relates to our system of belief. If you meet a person who says, "I believe in God," but does not accept Jesus Christ as Lord and Savior, they are not for you. If you get to know someone who says, "I read the Bible," but it is not God's word, here's some sound advice: do not try to convert them; kindly leave them where you found them.

Today's Push
You will be shocked to find out what people believe. If you are prayerfully seeking the Lord for a spouse, do not be afraid to ask people what they think about God, Jesus Christ, the church, and the Bible. Their answers may surprise you.

If they do not believe what you believe as a Christian, today's study passage gives you the right to walk off and not look back.

READ - St. Mark 16:16

Today's Prayer
Eternal God our Father, please place people in my path who are in love with you regarding relationships. Continue guiding me in this area because, without you, I am lost, but with you, I have the light of life.

In The Name of Jesus, Amen.

WEEK 5: Help Me Handle It When There's Somebody for Everybody but Me!

Day 4

BE CAREFUL TOO MUCH, TOO SOON CAN BE DANGEROUS!

Today's Passage
Be ye not unequally yoked together with unbelievers: for what fellowship hath righteousness with unrighteousness? And what communion hath light with darkness? (2 Cor. 6:14, KJV)

Today's Point To Practice
A devotional week on the subject of relationships would be incomplete if we did not mention the topic of sex. Let's face it: sex is everywhere these days. It's on the cover of magazines in the local supermarket, on TV, and in the music lyrics, we hear and sing occasionally. Yet, sexual intimacy is God's idea and should be done His way.

With this in mind, the Bible is careful to warn believers regarding the sins of the flesh, such as lust, adultery, fornication, and lascivious behavior. The problem that many singles run into is that too much is given too fast in this area, and it leaves a trail of sin, hurt feelings, damaged emotions, and ruptured relationships.

To have it done God's way, a Christian couple should wait until after they are married to embrace and involve themselves in sexual intimacy. Any other way will always prove to be too much, too soon.

Today's Push
Remember this: if you keep allowing people to sample your grapes who you are not married to , you won't have enough grapes to make a good bottle of wine when you get married. You are worth waiting for!

READ - Hebrews 13:4

Today's Prayer
Lord Jesus, teach me how to wait with you in this area of my walk. Help me not to get in your way, move too soon, or make foolish mistakes because I failed to wait for your guidance, wisdom, and blessing.

In The Name of Jesus, Amen.

WEEK 5: Help Me Handle It When There's Somebody for Everybody but Me!

Day 5

IF YOU WALK IN THE LIGHT, WHAT'S DARK WON'T LAST LONG!

Today's Passage
Be ye not unequally yoked together with unbelievers: for what fellowship hath righteousness with unrighteousness? And what communion hath light with darkness? (2 Cor. 6:14, KJV)

Today's Point To Practice
Not long ago, I witnessed something that, for our current culture, was a natural Christian phenomenon. What was it you ask? I performed a wedding for two young people, and both of them were virgins and proud of it. During their private vow exchange with one another, they both mentioned how they had never been sexually intimate with anyone. It was totally beautiful! There was not a dry eye in the entire place.

After the ceremony, while taking pictures, I could not help but ask them how they could do it. They blushed, grinned sheepishly, and said, "Pastor, if you walk in the light, what's dark won't last long." Here's the truth of the matter: They had both been tempted. To be tempted is human, but to overcome temptation is the result of a believer's walk with the Lord!

Today's Push
We do not often celebrate abstinence or commemorate celibacy; however, walking with the Lord intimately and closely gives us the strength to make it happen. With this in mind, remember this and hold on to it: "If you walk in the light, what's dark won't last long!"

READ-1 Cor. 7:7-9

Today's Prayer
Merciful Master, thank you for being the light of my life! Without you, I could not handle the darkness that sometimes comes my way. But, with you on my side, walking with you keeps me in the light!

In The Name of Jesus, Amen.

WEEK 5: Help Me Handle It When There's Somebody for Everybody but Me!

Day 6

IF GOD DID NOT SEND YOU, I'M NOT AVAILABLE!

Today's Passage
Be ye not unequally yoked together with unbelievers: for what fellowship hath righteousness with unrighteousness? And what communion hath light with darkness? (2 Cor. 6:14, KJV)

Today's Point To Practice
The real key to handling the reality of waiting on a spouse if you are single is not in isolation but in dedication. In other words, it is found in the fact that there is no time for foolishness with those who do not take their walk with Jesus Christ seriously.

Not long ago, while walking through a mall in Oklahoma, I stopped at a T-shirt stand in the store's center. They had all kinds of shirts for sale, but one shirt made a statement that stuck with me. No, it was not a Cowboys jersey or a Saints hoodie. It was a simple black-and-white T-shirt that said, "If God did not send you, I'm not available."

What a statement about their love for the Lord for those looking to handle dating as Christians!

Today's Push
For Singles Only: God knows what you need, who you need, and when you need that special person the most. Trust in the Lord with your life; He will help you handle it.

READ-Psalms 119:11

Today's Prayer
O God, thank you for allowing a person like me to walk with a God like you. Please continue being patient and merciful with me when my steps are not as large as yours. And thank you for becoming who I am in Jesus Christ so that your steps look just like mine.

God, I only want the people you have sent my way in my life.

In The Name of Jesus, Amen.

WEEK 5: Help Me Handle It When There's Somebody for Everybody but Me!

Day 7

TO BE SINGLE DOES NOT MEAN YOU HAVE TO BE LONELY!

Today's Passage
Be ye not unequally yoked together with unbelievers: for what fellowship hath righteousness with unrighteousness? And what communion hath light with darkness? (2 Cor. 6:14, KJV)

Today's Point To Practice
A great misnomer floating around secular and sacred circles must be put to rest. The rumor is that all single people are lonely. This is just not true at all! Single saints may be alone, but they are not lonely. Why? Because they are alone and have some good company.

Deacon Howard Mills was one of the oldest living men in the Antioch Missionary Baptist Church congregation in Beaumont, Texas, where I have been blessed to be a Pastor. While visiting with him one day, I asked him if he ever gets lonely. His reply took me by surprise. He said, "Pastor, I'm going to be a man until the day I die. There are some days I miss having a good wife and companion. Being single ain't always easy. But when I feel a little lonely, I just remember being alone with some good company....He never leaves me by myself!"

Today's Push
Falling in love with Jesus Christ is the best thing anyone will ever do in a lifetime. He is a company keeper, an ever-present Savior, and an always-present friend!

READ - St. John 15:15

Today's Prayer
Jesus, as I pray this petition, I want you to know that you mean everything to me. Thank you for helping me handle life when lonely moments come my way. I honor who you are and praise you for everything you mean to me.

In The Name of Jesus, Amen.

WEEK 6: Help Me Handle My Marriage When There's No Wine Left

Day 1

YOUR WINE IS SWEET, SO ENJOY IT WHILE IT LAST!

Our Passage of Study
When the ruler of the feast had tasted the water that was made wine and knew not whence it was (but the servants who drew the water knew;) the governor of the feast called the bridegroom,

And saith unto him, Every man at the beginning doth set forth good wine; and when men have well drunk, then that which is worse: but thou hast kept the good wine until now (St. John 2:9-11).

Today's Parable
It was one of the most extravagant weddings I had ever officiated. The cathedral of the church looked like something out of a magazine. The wedding coordinators and decorators transformed our old building into Buckingham's Palace. The Bridesmaids were stunning, the Groomsmen were handsome, and the guests were a dignified gathering of the who's who from around the region. After the wedding, a white horse and carriage were waiting outside to transport the newly married couple from the church to the hotel where the reception was being held, along with a motorcycle cop to handle traffic control.

The hotel lobby was filled with ice sculptors and a 28-piece jazz ensemble. Champagne was everywhere, and the party was on and popping! And did someone mention cake? When I say, I have never in my life seen a cake so beautiful! It was something that the Food Network could not replicate. When the night was over, the young couple flew to a remote island in the Netherlands, where they honeymooned. They returned to the States and endured marriage for two years and eight months!

All too often, people get married looking for "happily ever after," and it does not exist until you have been through valleys called "heartache," seasons of "what did I get myself into?" and a place called "I can't do this anymore."

To be clear, Christian marriage is a covenant relationship between a man and a woman who, through their love for Jesus Christ, seek to show the world what a reasonable facsimile of Christ and the Church looks like. In our study passage this week, we will explore the radical truths in Jesus' first miracle: He takes water and makes it wine at a wedding.

All marriages take a journey with the Lord, which involves dealing with times when you need help because your marriage has no wine left.

WEEK 6: Help Me Handle My Marriage When There's No Wine Left

Today's Prayer

Heavenly Father, today, heal, help, and hope every marital relationship that is under attack or that struggles. Let the fruit of your love be so prevalent in every Christian marriage until they show the world what real love is like.

In The Name of Jesus, Amen.

WEEK 6: Help Me Handle My Marriage When There's No Wine Left

Day 2

GOD WILL ALLOW YOUR MARRIAGE TO RUN OUT OF WINE!

Today's Passage
When the ruler of the feast had tasted the water that was made wine, and knew not whence it was: (but the servants which drew the water knew;) the governor of the feast called the bridegroom,

And saith unto him, Every man at the beginning doth set forth good wine; and when men have well drunk, then that which is worse: but thou hast kept the good wine until now (St. John 2:9-11).

Today's Point To Practice
If you still need to read the above story, do so immediately. It will take about a minute and thirty seconds for you to do so. Now that you have read it, did you notice in the narrative that they had plenty of wine at first? However, throughout the party, their wine ran out.

Please understand this: the same thing occurs in marriages worldwide over time. The wine runs out. Chivalry dies. The kitchen closes—the Bedroom struggles. Communication becomes hard. Forgiveness seems impossible. Third-party intrusions get in the way. And, the wine that you once had, you no longer have. He used to open the door; she used to cook all the time; He used to talk your ear off, but now he's mute and cannot communicate. She used to be hot and passionate with her intimacy, and now things are cold, and the bedroom gives you frostbite every time you walk into it.

Today's Push
Remember this, and please never forget it: Your marriage will run out of wine; however, just because it's empty does not mean God will let it stay that way. Marriages are tested, and the faithful couples reach the portal of new wine! So, stay focused no matter how empty your marriage feels because God is up to something in your relationship. READ - St. Matthew 24:13

Today's Prayer
God, today, my prayer is for couples who have run out of wine and cannot handle it. Lord, show them what your power is like so that they can discover the sufficiency of your grace and the boundless bliss of your mercy in their relationship.

In The Name of Jesus, Amen.

WEEK 6: Help Me Handle My Marriage When There's No Wine Left

Day 3

DON'T BE AFRAID TO ADMIT THAT YOUR MARRIAGE NEEDS A REFILL!

Today's Passage
When the ruler of the feast had tasted the water that was made wine, and knew not whence it was: (but the servants which drew the water knew;) the governor of the feast called the bridegroom,

And saith unto him, Every man at the beginning doth set forth good wine; and when men have well drunk, then that which is worse: but thou hast kept the good wine until now (St. John 2:9-11).

Today's Point To Practice
Sometimes, people fake it until they can make it. You can fake it with a co-worker that you do not care for. You can fake it when some family members get on your last nerve during a reunion picnic. However, when it comes to marriage, faking it does not work because you have to see your spouse every day. And, at some point, what is real will have to surface.

Here's today's lesson: When your marriage is empty, do not be afraid of it. Do not try to fix it or even cover it up. Admit that it is empty and needs to be refilled. WAIT, be careful who you admit your emptiness to. Let me recommend only admitting it to the Lord; at least you know you'll never hear it again.

Today's Push
You will only get a refill once you ask for one. Pretending to be full when your relationship is empty only prolongs your agony of being empty. Tell God about it, and you will discover that refills are on the house.

READ - St. Matthew 7:7-8

Today's Prayer
Lord Jesus, thank you for being the God who always answers our prayers. Thank you for helping me handle life when things are beyond my control. May your name always be praised in my heart for your goodness.

In The Name of Jesus, Amen.

WEEK 6: Help Me Handle My Marriage When There's No Wine Left

Day 4

DON'T LET THE DEVIL HAVE YOUR MARRIAGE!

Today's Passage
When the ruler of the feast had tasted the water that was made wine, and knew not whence it was: (but the servants which drew the water knew;) the governor of the feast called the bridegroom,

And saith unto him, Every man at the beginning doth set forth good wine; and when men have well drunk, then that which is worse: but thou hast kept the good wine until now (St. John 2:9-11).

Today's Point To Practice
A few years ago, a divorced couple from our congregation came to me for counseling. Of course, I wanted to know why they were coming to me if they had already been divorced for a couple of years. I whispered a prayer when they arrived and immediately asked them why they came to see me. Their answer was most interesting. The gentleman said, "Pastor, we do not understand what has happened to us. We have come full circle. We have gone from loving to hating each other back to loving each other and need help. What's going on with our relationship?"

I told this couple that no football player gets tackled on the field standing by the Gatorade jug! Only when players try to carry the ball are they hit and tackled ferociously. To make it clear, when you say "I do," demons in hell are assigned to you for one reason, and that is to destroy your covenant and to change your mind from "I do" to "I do not." They were so close and good friends now because no covenant was present. In other words, they are no longer carrying the ball. They are just standing by the proverbial Gatorade jug.

Today's Push
If you let the devil have your marriage, he will take it! The choice is yours. Let the devil have it or decide to fight for it.

READ - James 4:7

Today's Prayer
O God of Heaven and earth, do not let the enemy have anything you died for me to possess. Thank you for victory over the demonic attack from your throne to my home.

In The Name of Jesus, Amen.

WEEK 6: Help Me Handle My Marriage When There's No Wine Left

Day 5

DO WHATEVER IT TAKES!

Today's Passage
When the ruler of the feast had tasted the water that was made wine, and knew not whence it was: (but the servants which drew the water knew;) the governor of the feast called the bridegroom,

And saith unto him, Every man at the beginning doth set forth good wine; and when men have well drunk, then that which is worse: but thou hast kept the good wine until now (St. John 2:9-11).

Today's Point To Practice
One of the most exciting things in the story recorded in John 2 is when they run out of wine and need more of it, Jesus sends them to get water. The problem with such a request is that water is not needed to make wine. You need grapes to make wine, not water. Yet, Jesus tells them to go and get water. The idea behind this request is that sometimes, in order to get what the Lord has for you, it requires that you function by faith and do whatever it takes.

When it comes to saving a marriage that is really in trouble, you have to do whatever it takes to make it work—suffering for things that are not your fault, struggling with habits that are not areas of your human deficiency, and apologizing for things that you did not do. Marriage is hard work, it's not for the faint of heart. However, it is for the faithful believer who can say, "For Christ, I live, and for Christ, I will die," and mean it. Real marriages are made up of two sinners who sin and somehow, through the grace of God, find a way to do whatever it takes to stay until one of them dies.

Today's Push
Here's the truth: Marriage is for those willing to sacrifice whatever it takes to keep it. In short, marriage is for losers, and there's no way around it. The great news about losing is that we lose to win! READ - Col. 3:23

Today's Prayer
Father in Heaven, there are times when I try to handle matters on my own, and I am asking you right now to forgive me. Yet, Lord, I want to ask you for the strength to do my part, and you do everything else. Help me do whatever it takes, O God.

In The Name of Jesus, Amen.

WEEK 6: Help Me Handle My Marriage When There's No Wine Left

Day 6

NEW WINE IS ALWAYS THE BEST!

Today's Passage
When the ruler of the feast had tasted the water that was made wine, and knew not whence it was: (but the servants which drew the water knew;) the governor of the feast called the bridegroom,

And saith unto him, Every man at the beginning doth set forth good wine; and when men have well drunk, then that which is worse: but thou hast kept the good wine until now (St. John 2:9-11).

Today's Point To Practice
The best news in this week's passage is that the story begins with wine and ends with wine. The difference between the two wines presented in the story is that they started with the wine they made and it ran out. However, the last wine that they were given was different from theirs. It was the wine Jesus had made. It was the wine that was given and not earned. It was the wine that started and never stopped. It was the wine that was sweeter and better than any other wine they had ever had before. The wine was so sweet until the governor of the feast said, "… You've saved the good wine until now.…"

Many times in marriage, we love each other "because of" and not "in-spite of". When people get married they do so "because-of" things that their spouse will do, say, buy, listen to, and assist with. However, this love shifts. It changes. In many instances, what attracted you to your spouse dissipates, dissolves or even dies over a period of time. When this occurs it leaves a marriage empty when it comes to having wine in the marital relationship. Marriages that grow to a place in spiritual maturity learn to love each other not "because-of" but, "In-spite of." In relationships like this forgiveness, tolerance, forbearance, patience, endurance and acceptance are dominant.

To love your spouse "because-of" is one thing, but to love them "in-spite" is something deeper and more meaningful and this is where the new wine can be found. With this in mind, new wine is always the best. The only way to get it is to endure until God graces you with it!

Today's Push
You only go from your wine to new wine after going through the shifts that are presented in our scripture reading for the week that look like this; from your wine to no wine, from no wine to needing wine, from needing wine to having God grace you with the best wine, which is the new

WEEK 6: Help Me Handle My Marriage When There's No Wine Left

wine. It's a process! It is a marital journey so trust in the Lord, hold God's hand and walk with Him.

READ-Eph. 5:21-33

Today's Prayer
Lord Jesus, I will fight to attain new wine if you want me to have it. May I ask you for the strength to endure and persevere until it comes?

In The Name of Jesus, Amen.

WEEK 6: Help Me Handle My Marriage When There's No Wine Left

Day 7

IT CAN LAST FOREVER!

Today's Passage
When the ruler of the feast had tasted the water that was made wine, and knew not whence it was: (but the servants which drew the water knew;) the governor of the feast called the bridegroom,

And saith unto him, Every man at the beginning doth set forth good wine; and when men have well drunk, then that which is worse: but thou hast kept the good wine until now (St. John 2:9-11).

Today's Point To Practice
LaVert and Shelley Mollett renewed their vows on their 50th anniversary. On their special day, they both took turns sharing their intimate thoughts of what their 50-year journey had been like with each other. Brother Shelley went first, and when he finished, there was no dry eye. He stood before a huge crowd and told everyone present that his wife had to put up with his foolishness because he was a rascal she had to handle, but she did it. He admitted to running the streets and was open about not always being truthful. He even told us that he did not always trust his wife, so for years, he looked at her with a watchful eye, waiting for her to try and take his money.

The blessing came when Shelley told his wife that she was God's gift to him, and when he passed from time and would slip into eternity if she was still alive, he wanted to hold her hand. Since that day, both Shelley and LaVert have passed away. They are now with God, resting until the trumpet sounds in the rapture. The one thing every married couple can gain from their marital relationship is this: it can last forever!

Today's Push
The marriage that lasts is the marriage that simply never quits. READ - St. Mark 10:7-9

Today's Prayer
Gracious God of glory and goodness, help my relationships be healthy and happy is my sincere prayer. May those people you have placed in my life to whom I am connected remain with me until we meet you face-to-face on the other side.

In The Name of Jesus, Amen.

WEEK 7: Help Me Handle It When I'm Sick of It

Day 1

CHANGE ISN'T BAD IT IS NECESSARY!

Our Passage of Study
So Hannah rose up after they had eaten in Shiloh and after they had drunk. Now Eli, the priest, sat upon a seat by a post of the temple of the LORD. And she *was* in bitterness of soul, and prayed unto the LORD, and wept sore (1 Sam. 1:9-10, KJV).

Today's Parable
There comes a time in every Christian's life when change is not just necessary but essential. It happens when you find yourself surrounded by jealous people who pull you down, envious people who plot evil plans, and hateful people who are poisonous. It takes place when you have tried to be the bigger person, you have prayed and tried, and still, things do not get better; they get worse, forcing you to say, "I'm sick of it!"

It's the fall of 1989, and I'm employed with Harris County Housing Authority in Houston, Texas, and my job is nerve-shattering. My boss doesn't like me. I do not care about the work but need my check, so I'm doing my absolute best. To make matters worse, I'm starting to have health-related problems for the first time in my life. I pull into the parking lot twenty minutes early one Tuesday morning, ready to work. I grab my things, enter the building, get to my desk, and take a seat. Suddenly, a spirit came over me that made me say, "I'm sick of it!" I could not go any further. I could not pretend to be content anymore. I was ready for change, which would take place right then! One of the greatest mistakes any Christian could ever make is to take the trash from an old season of your life into a new one. As you read this book, I pray that you are entering a new life season. With this in mind, it makes no sense for you to leave the prior season of your life and walk into a new season with things that need to be changed, and you do not make an effort to change them.
You are sick of some things in your life right now, and now is your chance to make some life-changing decisions that will change the scope of your life forever!

Today's Prayer
Lord Jesus, thank you for making me determined to know when change is necessary. God, I know and realize that you are on my side. Your presence gives me comfort and consolation. Help me, O God, make the right decisions at the right time so that what comes from my decisions are blessings that come from you.

In The Name of Jesus, Amen.

WEEK 7: Help Me Handle It When I'm Sick of It

Day 2

God's Word for You Today: RISE!

Today's Passage
So Hannah rose up after they had eaten in Shiloh, and after they had drunk. Now Eli the priest sat upon a seat by a post of the temple of the LORD. And she *was* in bitterness of soul, and prayed unto the LORD, and wept sore (1 Sam. 1:9-10, KJV).

Today's Point To Practice
You may not be able to choose your conditions, but you can make some positive adjustments while dealing with them. In our Bible story, Hannah faces many problems that make her life uncomfortable. She has an internal problem; she is barren and cannot have children. Her external adversary, Peninnah, constantly confronts her. She has a relational problem in that she has a good man, but he just does not understand her pain or private predicaments at all. One day, while faced with all three problems, Hannah does something God graced her with the volitional prerogative to do. Our study passage for the week records it on this wise, "So Hannah rose….." This is so powerful and poignant. Despite her conditions and circumstances, Hannah decided to rise!

READ - St. Mark 16:15-16

Today's Push
Right now, you may be faced with conditions that look and feel unfavorable. You may be confronting issues and challenges that no one completely comprehends. The great news about what you are dealing with is that God graced you with the volitional ability to rise, to get up, and to move on, no matter how difficult this may be. Remember that Hannah was not commanded to rise; she decided to do so, and the rest is history.

Just like Hannah rose, you can too! Here's the word for today: Rise!

Today's Prayer
God, you never promised us ideal conditions and pleasant circumstances. However, you did bless us with the ability to make sound decisions. Today, in your presence, through your power, and with your divine permission, I have chosen to rise! Lord, I rise over demonic attacks, negative thoughts, worry, stress, anxiety, and evil from any source.

In The Name of Jesus, Amen.

WEEK 7: Help Me Handle It When I'm Sick of It

Day 3

WHAT'S BITTER WILL SOON BECOME BETTER!

Today's Passage
So Hannah rose up after they had eaten in Shiloh, and after they had drunk. Now Eli the priest sat upon a seat by a post of the temple of the LORD. And she *was* in bitterness of soul, and prayed unto the LORD, and wept sore (1 Sam. 1:9-10, KJV).

Today's Point To Practice
Not long ago, while sharing a movie with my kids, they introduced me to a candy called Sour Patch Straws. I like snacking on Milk Duds, Now & Laters, or some plain ole M&M's. Nevertheless, I gave their candy a try, and it was horrible! It was bitter and nasty, so I got rid of them. My kids looked at me and said, "Daddy, you have to hold on to them long enough for the bitterness to leave and the sweet taste to come." There are times when walking with God can be like that. As a believer in Christ things can be bitter. But if you can endure the moment and persevere through the season, what is now bitter can become better! The Bible carefully mentions Hannah's "….bitterness of soul…." This Hebrew idiom references circumstances that cause discomfort, discouragement, and disgust in one way or another. This is how her story begins; however, it is not how her narrative ends. She encounters the power of redemptive reversal from God. The Lord takes what is bitter and makes things better!

READ - Exodus 15:22-26, KJV

Today's Prayer
Lord, I am not complaining, but I must be honest: sometimes my conditions are bitter. Life hurts from time to time, and I struggle with it. Today, O God, as I pray, I humbly ask you to help me handle the bitter things by knowing and believing that with your grace and love, they can soon improve. I thank you, Lord Jesus, for the things you have allowed in my life that have been bitter. My hard times have caused me to trust you more. And I thank you so much for the things in my life that you have made better. Knowing that you can take my bitter days and give me better conditions makes my heart glad because my God is always in control.

In The Name of Jesus, Amen.

WEEK 7: Help Me Handle It When I'm Sick of It

Day 4

PRAY YOUR WAY THROUGH!

Today's Passage
So Hannah rose up after they had eaten in Shiloh, and after they had drunk. Now Eli the priest sat upon a seat by a post of the temple of the LORD. And she *was* in bitterness of soul, and prayed unto the LORD, and wept sore (1 Sam. 1:9-10, KJV).

Today's Point To Practice
While watching some bodybuilders train at the gym not long ago, I noticed the advice their trainer was giving each of them as they lifted on the flat bench. The trainer said, "You will only see results if you press your way through. If you do not press your way through, you will not see the chest muscles you hope to gain." Today's point to practice is not about bench pressing, but it is about prayerfully pushing! Sometimes, you will only see the results you want to see in life if you pray your way through.

Hannah "….prayed unto the Lord…" The word used for *pray*ing in the passage means to pray continually. It also means to pray silently! Here's the point to practice, don't stop praying! Pray when you feel like it; pray when you do not feel up to it; and pray when it seems nothing is happening. Pray your way through!

READ - 1 Thessalonians 5:17

Today's Prayer
O Lord my God, forgive me for becoming slothful in my prayers to you. There are times I pray fervently, and other times I stop praying because I do not see the desired results. Please remove my doubt and give me more faithfulness. Help me pray my way through things, especially when it seems like nothing is changing. Teach me, O Lord, to understand that when you are not changing my conditions when I pray, you are changing me amid my conditions, so prayer still works. Please help me, Lord Jesus, pray my way through.

In The Name of Jesus, Amen.

WEEK 7: Help Me Handle It When I'm Sick of It

Day 5

YESTERDAY I CRIED!

Today's Passage
So Hannah rose up after they had eaten in Shiloh, and after they had drunk. Now Eli the priest sat upon a seat by a post of the temple of the LORD. And she *was* in bitterness of soul, and prayed unto the LORD, and wept sore (1 Sam. 1:9-10, KJV).

Today's Point To Practice
Our study passage for the week concludes like this, "Hannah....wept sore." The idea behind such a statement is that Hannah cried until she could not cry anymore. Have you ever been there before? It can happen when a loved one dies, when a divorce is final, or when a disease causes chaos in your body. In this case, it happened because Hannah had a physical problem; she could not bear children. The great news of today's lesson is that God gave us tears to cry with. In fact, we have lacrimatory glands so that we can cry when we need to. But, the celebration in this story is that tears come with a limit. There are only so many tears that you can cry. This gives you the right to say, "I'm through crying over that," or better put, "Yesterday I cried!"

I do not know what tears you have had to cry lately. But I know this: the tears that flow today will not always flow. They will eventually cease, and things will turn in your favor.

READ-Psalms 30:5

Today's Prayer
God, no one knows the tears I silently cry but you. No one knows the secret struggles that cause me discomfort but you. You know me, O Lord, and I thank you for wiping my tears, lifting my head, and keeping me sane. King Jesus, help me live with my tears, knowing that weeping may endure for a night, but joy comes in the morning.

In The Name of Jesus, Amen.

WEEK 7: Help Me Handle It When I'm Sick of It

Day 6

I'VE HAD ENOUGH!

Today's Passage
So Hannah rose up after they had eaten in Shiloh, and after they had drunk. Now Eli the priest sat upon a seat by a post of the temple of the LORD. And she *was* in bitterness of soul, and prayed unto the LORD, and wept sore (1 Sam. 1:9-10, KJV).

Today's Point To Practice
To be sick of a set of circumstances is one thing, but to say "I've had enough" is different. When you have had enough, it suggests you have reached your limit and even exceeded your maximum. It means you have gone as far as you plan to go, and something has to give. Mark 5:21-34 tells the story of a woman with an issue with blood. She has suffered twelve years working with doctors, but instead of getting better, she got worse. Her money runs out, her health is getting worse, and she gets to a point where she has had enough. She gets up and goes to Jesus and, due to the size of the crowd, can only touch the hem of His garment. Of course, she is healed by that one touch. But here's the point: she got to a place where she could say, "I've had enough!"

Here's the point to practice: When you reach the place where you have had enough, be mindful that God is still God, and He is still in control.

READ- Matthew 17:14-21

Today's Prayer
Lord Jesus, I am fed up with some things in my life, and I have taken all that I plan to take. I have had enough. Grace me with the power, strength, and wherewithal to seek you like never before and to hold on to your unchanging hand because you will not fail me.

In The Name of Jesus, Amen.

WEEK 7: Help Me Handle It When I'm Sick of It

Day 7

WATCH GOD CHANGE IT!

Today's Passage
So Hannah rose up after they had eaten in Shiloh, and after they had drunk. Now Eli the priest sat upon a seat by a post of the temple of the LORD. And she *was* in bitterness of soul, and prayed unto the LORD, and wept sore (1 Sam. 1:9-10, KJV).

Today's Point To Practice
Nothing comes in contact with God and remains the same. He changes things. If God encounters a bucket of water, He changes it into wine. If the Lord runs into a blind man, his sight is restored. If God meets a crazy man in a tomb, that same man will leave that graveyard sane and sound in his right mind. Here's the point: our God changes things! It is why you are a believer right now. He has made some changes in your life that will remain forever.

With this in mind, here is the point to practice. When you are sick of it and do not know what to do about it, turn it over to the Lord and watch God change it.

Here's a beautiful devotional question to ponder as we conclude sharing our study verse for the week: has the Lord ever changed anything for you? Have you ever watched God turn things around? The great news about our God's past is that He can do it again if He's done it before!

READ - St. John 2:1-11

Today's Prayer
Lord, my prayer today is for you to give me the patience and the discipline to watch you work it out for me when I cannot fix it alone. Thank you for my testimony, which says I have watched you work things out for me before, and I know that if you have done it before, you have the power to do it again. Thank you, Jesus, for helping me handle it when I reached the point where I was sick of it. Help me endure and strengthen me to overcome.

In The Name of Jesus, Amen.

WEEK 8: Help Me Handle It When It's Too Much for Me to Handle!

Day 1

IF IT'S TOO MUCH FOR YOU, IT'S JUST RIGHT FOR HIM!

Our Passage of Study
Come unto me, all ye that labour and are heavy laden, and I will give you rest. Take my yoke upon you, and learn of me; for I am meek and lowly in heart: and ye shall find rest unto your souls. For my yoke is easy, and my burden is light (St. Matt. 11:28-30).

Today's Parable
Birthday parties are big these days. Some people celebrate their birthdays the entire month long. I was once invited to a huge birthday celebration, which was a bash. No, it was not Deon Sanders' all-white bash in Dallas or a Diddy party thrown by Sean Combs. However, it was the party of the year. It was the birthday party of a five-year-old girl from our church, who I will leave in complete anonymity.

All of her friends wore gold and white, her favorite colors. Her backyard was packed with friends and family, and her mom was in the kitchen cooking all her favorites, including praline cups made from scratch! However, the guest of honor was sitting in the house frustrated, trying to fix a doll that was a gift of hers that was supposed to walk, talk, and dance.

Frustration, irritation, and agitation had set in. She had pulled one arm off the doll, and tears started falling. I went to help her out, but her Father stopped me. He said, "Pastor, let me see you for a moment." I stopped in my tracks and headed to the couch he was resting on. He told me quietly that he had told her to bring him her doll when she opened the box. But she did not do it. He said I told her to bring it to me four times, and she refused. If you help her, she will never learn to bring what's broken to me. Thanks for your help, but I've got this!

I watched the birthday girl the whole time. She missed her entire party trying to fix her doll. Her guests ate her food, sang Happy Birthday, and enjoyed her cake while she sat wrestling with her doll. Finally, after utterly dismantling her new baby doll, she came running to her daddy and said, "Daddy, I can't do it. Fix it for me!" I watched the whole scene as if it were a movie on Netflix! He picked her up, fixed her doll, and pulled out a separate birthday cake and some food that he had saved her. She sat on his lap enjoying, grinning, and tearing open the other gifts that were hers to enjoy.

Here's a great devotional question for you to ponder: How long are you going to try to fix what's broken in your life before you run to God and say, "Daddy, I can't do it. Fix it for me?" Here's

WEEK 8: Help Me Handle It When It's Too Much for Me to Handle!

the good news: When you make the decision to run to Him, you will discover that He can fix what you are unable and inept to repair.

Hear the words of Jesus in our study passage from the week. "Come unto me, all ye that labour and are heavy laden, and I will give you rest. Take my yoke upon you, and learn of me; for I am meek and lowly in heart: and ye shall find rest unto your souls. For my yoke is easy, and my burden is light." If it's too big for you, it's suitable for Him!

Today's Prayer
Lord, some things in my life are just too big for me to handle. I have tried my best to tackle them but to no avail. Forgive me for not trusting you with my trouble and depending on you like I should have. Right now, I give you everything that is too much for me because I know it is just right for you.

In The Name of Jesus, Amen.

WEEK 8: Help Me Handle It When It's Too Much for Me to Handle!

Day 2

EVERYONE NEEDS IT, BUT NOT EVERYBODY QUALIFIES!

Today's Passage
Come unto me, all ye that labour and are heavy laden, and I will give you rest. Take my yoke upon you, and learn of me; for I am meek and lowly in heart: and ye shall find rest unto your souls. For my yoke is easy, and my burden is light (St. Matt. 11:28-30).

Today's Point To Practice
When you examine the verses that are listed for our study this week, you will discover something very interesting. Everyone is welcome to "come unto me," as the scripture teaches, but not everyone qualifies. According to the truths of the text, only those who meet a certain set of criteria are welcomed. Look carefully at the verse again. It explicitly states that those who "....labour and are heavy ladened..." should come. These terms are agrarian in that they refer to a beast of the field with a load that is too much for them to pull or carry. Jesus says bring those loads to me, and I will give you rest.

If your load is light and you can handle it, then you don't need today's lesson. But, if you are tired and worn out (labored) and your load is too much to bear (heavy laden), you fit the description of those the Lord wants to help.

Here's a rather nosy question that I want to ask you, and it's personal. How heavy is your load?

Today's Push
What sense does it make to carry your load alone when you have a God who is a heavy load bearer and a heavy load sharer? Let God have your load and move on!

READ - Psalms 55:22

Today's Prayer
God of Heaven, today I approach you with every burden I have tried to carry, and I say to you right now, Lord, you can have each of them because I can do nothing with them.

In The Name of Jesus, Amen.

WEEK 8: Help Me Handle It When It's Too Much for Me to Handle!

Day 3

I WILL MEANS HE HEALS!

Today's Passage
Come unto me, all ye that labour and are heavy laden, and I will give you rest. Take my yoke upon you, and learn of me; for I am meek and lowly in heart: and ye shall find rest unto your souls. For my yoke is easy, and my burden is light (St. Matt. 11:28-30).

Today's Point To Practice
One of the greatest facets of the Lord's character is that He is a healer. God alone heals. All healing comes from the Lord. God is responsible for all healing, whether it be through surgery, a prescription from a pharmacy, or the ability of a local doctor. Jesus Christ is our healer!

With this in mind, we have one of the most hopeful passages in the Bible to study this week that should help you handle anything that life throws your way. Jesus declares an "I will" for us to shout about. You see, when God says I will, the devil can't stop it, the government can't block it, you can't change it, and your conditions do not derail or cancel it. The text says something amazing happens when you bring your tired, worn-out, burden-bearing self to God and leave everything with Him!

He gives you something that money cannot buy, and credit cannot charge. He says, "I will give you rest!"

Today's Push
Listen, if you need rest, you will have it when you trust God with your issues, conditions, circumstances, and situations. Trust Him now, and never doubt Him!

READ - Psalms 91:2

Today's Prayer
Eternal God, my Father, sometimes I need healing from the rest you provide. My sacred petition for you today is to ask for healing and rest that I know comes from you. Thank you for honoring this petition and hearing my cry.

In The Name of Jesus, Amen.

WEEK 8: Help Me Handle It When It's Too Much for Me to Handle!

Day 4

HIS REST IS YOUR GIFT!

Today's Passage
Come unto me, all ye that labour and are heavy laden, and I will give you rest. Take my yoke upon you, and learn of me; for I am meek and lowly in heart: and ye shall find rest unto your souls. For my yoke is easy, and my burden is light (St. Matt. 11:28-30).

Today's Point To Practice
Imagine for a moment God having a garage sale. (Wait, I know that this sounds crazy, but just keep reading before you close this book and laugh.) On one table, He has salvation. On another table, He offers justification, sanctification, imputation, expiation, and propitiation as a group sale. On another table, He has answered prayer, miracles, and even a mansion in Heaven.

But at the back of the garage sale, there is one very special item on the table marked "Special Item, Special Delivery." One passerby asked the Lord what this item was, and God smiled joyfully and said, "This one is my specialty. I use it when my children have grown weary in the well-doing, worn in their walk with me, weak in studying my word and weathered in their worship of me." The passerby asked, "Well, Lord, what is this special item?" Then, the Lord said, "This one is my rest! It is a gift, and I deliver it personally."

Today's Push
It is not a sin for you to rest! If you do not rest when you are worn out, He will "make you lie down…" It's easier for you to stop on your on than for the Lord to stop you. Rest! You deserve this gift from the Lord, and He delivers it personally.

READ - Psalms 127:2

Today's Prayer
O God, there are times I struggle with just resting. I pray that my temporal and eternal rest will only be found in you from this moment.

In The Name of Jesus, Amen.

WEEK 8: Help Me Handle It When It's Too Much for Me to Handle!

Day 5

GOOD NEWS, HE'S CARRYING YOU AND YOUR LOAD!

Today's Passage
Come unto me, all ye that labour and are heavy laden, and I will give you rest. Take my yoke upon you, and learn of me; for I am meek and lowly in heart: and ye shall find rest unto your souls. For my yoke is easy, and my burden is light (St. Matt. 11:28-30).

Today's Point To Practice
I was blessed to grow up in a household where both parents were present with me until they were called from labor to reward. My mother raised the children and cared for things at the house, and my dad worked daily. In fact, to the best of my recollection, he had about five jobs. He drove pharmaceutical trucks for McKesson; he Pastored the New Hope Church, often served as an evangelist and guest speaker, and traveled when needed. He was an entrepreneur who repossessed car engines and worked in the petrochemical industry, restoring heavy valve equipment and reselling the parts to local plants for economic gain.

With this in mind, he taught me the value of working by having me work with him occasionally. I would help him with these huge valves in the backyard. He would have me clean them with steel brushes and then load them onto his truck for delivery. I did fine with the cleaning, but loading those heavy valves was another story. I could not lift one of the valves on one occasion, and he got behind me. I grunted and strained, picked up the valve, and walked it to his truck without stopping. I was so proud of myself until I reached the truck, turned around, and saw my Father holding the entire valve with one hand!

You see, I had my hand on it, but his hand carried it. My Father carried my load the entire time!

Today's Push
Here's something for you to hold on to for the rest of your life as a believer in Jesus: our God is a heavy load bearer! Just when you think your hand is doing the work, look again. It is the Lord who is carrying you and your load. READ- Psalms 46:1

Today's Prayer
Lord Jesus Christ, there are times when my load is heavy. In those moments, times, and seasons, be my heavy load bearer and my heavy load sharer.

In The Name of Jesus, Amen.

WEEK 8: Help Me Handle It When It's Too Much for Me to Handle!

Day 6

LEARN THE LESSON, LEAVE THE PAIN!

Today's Passage
Come unto me, all ye that labour and are heavy laden, and I will give you rest. Take my yoke upon you, and learn of me; for I am meek and lowly in heart: and ye shall find rest unto your souls. For my yoke is easy, and my burden is light (St. Matt. 11:28-30).

Today's Point To Practice
When life wears you out, sin wears you thin, and human hurt gets the best of you, rest is what you need. However, if you are like many, finding rest isn't always easy because there are people attached to the pain that you have had to endure. Today's remedy is redemptive and simple: Rest comes to those in Christ who know how to learn the lesson and leave the pain.

In the mid-1980s, I watched my only sister, Nell, go through a rough life season. Marital challenges at the home front, coupled with issues that came at her from every direction the devil could throw a dart, made her life hell. I watched as she endured and found ways to overcome even when overwhelmed. I quickly noticed the key to her healing, strength, and endurance: she never dwelled on the negative; she just stayed with the positive. She stayed with the Lord! She had seen times that crushed her and caused pain, but she never complained. She just learned the lessons and left the pain!

Today's Push
If you hold onto your pain and the things that have caused it, life will make you bitter, mean, and harmful. Here is today's push for you, and if you practice it, you will discover it is helpful when you cannot handle it. Learn the lesson, and leave the pain.

READ-1 Samuel 30:6

Today's Prayer
Eternal God, my Father, no one on earth knows my real pain like you do. No one cares for me like you have, and no one has counted my tears the way you have. Today as I spend this moment with you, empower me to not hold grudges and to move on with the lessons my heartache has taught me.

In The Name of Jesus, Amen.

WEEK 8: Help Me Handle It When It's Too Much for Me to Handle!

Day 7

GOD WILL TAKE CARE OF YOU!

Today's Passage

Come unto me, all ye that labour and are heavy laden, and I will give you rest. Take my yoke upon you, and learn of me; for I am meek and lowly in heart: and ye shall find rest unto your souls. For my yoke is easy, and my burden is light (St. Matt. 11:28-30).

Today's Point To Practice

The last ten words of this passage found in verse thirty bless me the most. Here's why: Jesus does not say you will not have problems. He does not infer or suggest that you will not have any burdens. That is not one of His promises to those who follow Him. He does promise that His yoke is easy and His burden is light. You may ask yourself, what does this phrase mean? Here's what it means: I hope you retain and always remember it. His discipline for your life is bearable, and the heavy load that He permits is always manageable. It will never be too much for you to bear and will never be a burden you must carry alone. In August 2005, Hurricane Katrina struck the Gulf Coast, leaving the heavy weight and burden of destruction all over the crescent city of New Orleans and surrounding areas. Thousands lost millions of dollars in property damage, and millions suffered too much to chronicle. In short, it was a disaster. In the aftermath of the storm, I spoke to my good friend Dr. Fred Luter from the Franklin Avenue Baptist Church and asked him if there was anything that we could do to help. His answer blessed me incredibly! Dr. Luter said, "My brother, we will endure and return because the Lord is with us, and He will not put any more on us than we can bear. My brother, please pray for us and know that the Lord will take care of us."

Today's Push

In moments when life's burdens are heaviest, and trouble is at its worst, feelings of abandonment slip in under the radar and can leave you feeling like even God does not care. However, in moments like that, remember these words, and I pray that they bring you ease, comfort, and consolation: God will take care of you. READ - Isaiah 46:4

Today's Prayer

Lord Jesus, you have always been the kind of Shepherd who cares well for His own sheep. Thank you for taking care of me even when I was unaware of it. I thank you for being so kind, loving, caring, and strong!

In The Name of Jesus, Amen.

WEEK 9: Help Me Handle Enemies in Close Proximity!

Day 1

GOD SAYS, "I'VE INVITED YOUR ENEMIES!"!

Our Passage of Study
Thou preparest a table before me in the presence of mine enemies: thou anointest my head with oil; my cup runneth over (Psalms 23:5).

Today's Parable
A party is being prepared for you. It's a special celebration. It's a secret celebration. It's your party, but you cannot control the guest list. You find out that the celebration is going down, so you pick your outfit and let the host know who you would like to see: family, friends, cohorts, constituents, and cousins (not really kin, but those folks that you claim but are no relation to you).

You are picked up in a Maybach Limo G-16 stretch. You get into the car, and your sipping friends already have things going. You arrive at the party in Houston, and it's at the city's finest, St. Regis, where rooms are only $695.00 a night, and you are there for the weekend. The music for the party was the best, and the food was—well, it was prepared by a chef whose real name was hidden, but they called him Adonai for short.

When you arrive, he receives you. As you walk the red carpet, flashes of cameras snap pictures of you looking and feeling great; the host says, "You are about to have the time of your life! Everyone is here, and this thing will top all the parties these folks have ever seen." And I Hope You Don't Mind, I Invited Your Enemies Too!

You get to the table, and there they are:
- The Abuser, The User, The Loser
- The Liar, the Backbiter, and the Fighter
- The no-good backstabber
- The X that tried to ruin you
- The thief who took your money
- The rapist that no one knows about
- The joker that dropped you
- The person who tried to hurt you and succeeded
- The cheater, the slacker, the packer and the hater

They are at your table, and Adonai grins and says, "Have a seat, and let's get this party started!"

WEEK 9: Help Me Handle Enemies in Close Proximity!

Contrary to popular belief and opinion, God does not exempt His children from having enemies in close proximity. The enemies that do the most damage are those who God has permitted to be in your presence, in your face, and in your space from time to time. Think about it this way: if Jesus had Judas and Caesar had Brutus, you would have at least one person in close proximity, which means your life is no good!

The question is, how do you handle enemies that exist near you? That's what this week will be designed to empower you with.

Today's Prayer
Jesus, I often find myself in the company of those who do not have my best interest in mind. And there are times I have found myself angry and resentful toward them. Empower me with enough of who you are so that I can handle them the way you would.

In The Name of Jesus, Amen.

WEEK 9: Help Me Handle Enemies in Close Proximity!

Day 2

YOUR LIFE IS BEING GUARDED BY THE LORD!

Today's Passage
Thou preparest a table before me in the presence of mine enemies: thou anointest my head with oil; my cup runneth over (Psalms 23:5).

Today's Point To Practice
Some people make it a habit of keeping their enemies out of their faces. But according to this verse, God does exactly the opposite. But why? Consider it momentarily and ponder this interrogative while spending time with God today. Why does a good God prepare a table of blessings for you and invite your enemies to watch? There may be many reasonable answers for us to consider; however, one answer is for sure. God wants your closest enemies to know that he guards you!

What should make you happy is that your enemies only see you and cannot see God. This gives you an uneven advantage because you win not because of what you can do but because of what God can do for you that you cannot do for yourself!

Today's Push
Your enemies are present, but your God is more powerful than any foe you will ever face!

READ - Exodus 14:14

Today's Prayer
Lord, I approach you right now with a spirit of gratitude! I am thankful because you are on my side and don't just guide me; you guard me! Thank you for your protection, which never fails.

In The Name of Jesus, Amen.

WEEK 9: Help Me Handle Enemies in Close Proximity!

Day 3

GET OVER IT!

Today's Passage
Thou preparest a table before me in the presence of mine enemies: thou anointest my head with oil; my cup runneth over (Psalms 23:5).

Today's Point To Practice
Let's begin today by being completely transparent about people in your face who do not like you at all. They are irritating, agitating, frustrating, and nauseating. People like this can make you sick to your stomach. They are nerve-wracking, joy-stealing, and mind-disturbing. They can make the old you want to reach out and grab them. They can provoke you to use profanity, and to make matters even worse; they can make it easy for you to become vengeful, angry, evil, and mean. Have you ever been here before? If you were truthful and answered yes, help is in the next paragraph.

Your table of blessing is prepared in the presence of your enemies, so get over it! Get over the things they've said! Get over the damage they've done! Get over the time you wasted on them! Get over how they used you with your permission! Get over the calls you made, the money you spent, the prayers you prayed, and the things they have done to make your life a living hell! Get over it!

Today's Push
God allows your enemies to exist at your table of blessing, so get over it. If they were not present, your table would not exist! Stay focused on what's on the table for you, prepared by the hand of God, and know that there is more to come.

READ - Exodus 50:20

Today's Prayer
Jesus, today I want to give you a strange thanksgiving. I want to thank the people who turned their backs on me. When they turned from me, you extended your hand towards me. I want to thank the people who lied to me. When they lied to me, I discovered more of your truth. I want to thank you for the people who hurt me deeply. When they wounded me, you took the time to restore me, and right now, I am stronger than I have ever been. Thank you for my enemies!

In The Name of Jesus, Amen.

WEEK 9: Help Me Handle Enemies in Close Proximity!

Day 4

I WANT YOUR ENEMIES TO SEE MY FAVOR ON YOUR LIFE!

Today's Passage
Thou preparest a table before me in the presence of mine enemies: thou anointest my head with oil; my cup runneth over (Psalms 23:5).

Today's Point To Practice
Many wonderful things come from the Lord. The Bible says, "…every good and perfect gift comes from the Lord…" (James 1:17a). Love, peace, answered prayer, and divine provision also come from the Lord. Salvation, deliverance, healing, restoration, and transformation come from the Lord. Love, mercy, protection, and direction also come from the Lord. However, the most potent gift that comes from God to humankind is His favor.

The favor of the Lord is better defined in simple terms as grace. The term grace in both Hebrew and Greek translates as the English word favor. If you remember nothing from today's lesson, hold on to this: God's favor is a game changer! It gives without gaining, justifies without judging, bleeds without you bruising, and rises without you dying. God's favor lets you live with things that have caused others to die. His favor will let you succeed in areas that others have failed in. And His favor will cause you to be fruitful in places barren for everyone else.

This is why your enemies are permitted to exist in close range. God makes them look, observe, and notice the favor He has placed on their lives.

Today's Push
The purpose of God's favor in your life is to remind everyone, including your enemies, that He is on your side!

READ - Psalms 90:17

Today's Prayer
Heavenly Father, thank you for the unparalleled favor you have graciously granted me. I know I do not deserve it, but I would like to say thank you for it.

In The Name of Jesus, Amen.

WEEK 9: Help Me Handle Enemies in Close Proximity!

Day 5

YOU'RE AT THE TABLE, BUT YOU DON'T HAVE A TAB!

Today's Passage
Thou preparest a table before me in the presence of mine enemies: thou anointest my head with oil; my cup runneth over (Psalms 23:5).

Today's Point To Practice
Often, after a night of sharing in revival services, those who have labored and preached God's Word journey to a nearby restaurant for food and fellowship. Such was the case after completing a revival in the Alamo City of San Antonio a few years ago. The evening had been incredible, and our appetites were ready and raring to go. We arrived at a very nice steakhouse, retreated to a private dining area, and someone shouted, "Let the games begin!"

Initially, all you could hear was chatting and talking about what the Lord did in our midst during the service. However, when the food started arriving, there was no more chatter. Instead, the clicking and clacking of forks, spoons, and knives hit the flatware as the food began filling our stomachs. Our waiter brought us a dessert menu when the main course was over, and many of us indulged.

It's now time for us to leave and make our way home. However, the waiter did not bring us the bill. The host Pastor called the waiter over to us and inquired about the bill for the entire table. It was rather costly; some brothers ordered prime rib, while others enjoyed salmon from the sea and lobster from a freshwater gallery tank. But the waiter told our host Pastor that our entire table had been paid for by a secret patron who wanted to bless us. You see, we had a huge table but no tab!

Today's Push
The benefit of knowing the Lord as a Shepherd is the blessing of knowing that you may have a tab, but your God has already paid for it. When did He it pay for it, you ask? On a hill far away on an old rugged cross! He died to pay for every single thing you would ever need that would come from Him. READ - Col. 1:14

Today's Prayer
Thank you, O God, for paying for my sins on the cross. I will forever be indebted to you for what you have done for me.

In The Name of Jesus, Amen.

WEEK 9: Help Me Handle Enemies in Close Proximity!

Day 6

GRACE WORKS FOR THEM LIKE IT WORKS FOR YOU!

Today's Passage
Thou preparest a table before me in the presence of mine enemies: thou anointest my head with oil; my cup runneth over (Psalms 23:5).

Today's Point To Practice
In the Hebrew culture of the first century, there were no chairs at a table used for dining. However, there was space for people to recline to eat. When the Lord prepares your table, He does so with it in the presence of your enemies. One of the reasons for this is to communicate to them a timeless truth that no Christian should ever forget. If God's grace works for us, it can also be sufficient for your enemies too.

Today's Push
God's grace is not just for the holy. It is for the unholy, the sinner, the drunkard, the thief, the rapist, the liar, the backslider, and even the murderer. It is for anyone who will bring their sins to the cross and leave them there.

READ - Rev. 22:17

Today's Prayer
Unto thee O God do I place my trust. Thankfully, I approach this moment to thank you for the grace that saved me and for the same grace that saves others who are like I used to be.

In The Name of Jesus, Amen.

WEEK 9: Help Me Handle Enemies in Close Proximity!

Day 7

SHOW THEM WHAT OVERFLOW LOOKS LIKE!

Today's Passage
Thou preparest a table before me in the presence of mine enemies: thou anointest my head with oil; my cup runneth over (Psalms 23:5).

Today's Point To Practice
How do you describe living in the overflow? I suggest that it looks like a beautiful portrait of you. Are you rich, poor, or middle class? I know the Lord has cared for you all of your life, and you have every need met in Him.

If you want to encourage yourself, sit down with a notepad and pen. Ponder just a moment how much the Lord has done for you. Trust me when I say this: the more you think about it, the better you will feel.

Compiling such a list will help you recall and remember the many manifold blessings the Lord has bestowed upon you and know that He did it in a place where your enemies were invited to watch.

Today's Push
Find a mirror, look at yourself in the face, and realize that the favor of the Lord is staring back at you! You are what an overflow seems like.

READ - Proverbs 3:10

Today's Prayer
God of dominance and dominion, I thank you for preparing my table of blessing in the presence of my enemies. May your hand perpetually lead, guide, and direct the affairs of the life that you give me until I pass from time and enter eternity.

In The Name of Jesus, Amen.

WEEK 10: Help Me Handle It When I Need a Refill!

Day 1

PARKED CARS DO NOT NEED MORE GAS FOR THE JOURNEY THAT LIES AHEAD!

Our Passage of Study
And be not drunk with wine, wherein is excess; but be filled with the Spirit; (Eph. 5:18).

Today's Parable
Many linguists argue that if a word or phrase remains in a culture for forty years or more, its meaning shifts tremendously. For example, crack used to be a hole in the pavement; weed was once a reference to wild grass that had to be pulled on your hands and knees from the flower bed; a cell was a biological construct; and the phrase "fill it up" was used when you pulled into a full-service gas station in the 1970s and needed a refill.

My Father knew a kind man named Mr. Ben. He owned the Gulf filling station in the shadow of the Houston Astrodome. My mother wouldn't get gas every day or even every week; she would wait to get a fill-up. She would take all possible measures to make her gas stretch. She would turn off the air conditioning, lower the windows, and, if need be, turn the radio off to save on gas. But just before she ran out, we would make our way over to Mr. Ben's Gulf Station. She would pull into the station and cross those black bell cables resting on the ground that would sound the bell.

Mr. Ben would say, "Mrs. Barbara, how can I help you?" And she would speak with great passion and enthusiasm, "Fill it up because I need a refill!"

Sometimes, even the strongest believers run empty and need a refill. The question that beckons us to consider its response is how do you handle it when you're empty, and no one knows it? What do you do when you need more from the Lord because you are empty?

Here is the purpose of this week's study: Hold fast to Ephesians 5:18 as we look to grow from its truth all week long.

Today's Prayer
Jesus, I'm empty, and you know it. I'm so busy helping others that I sometimes neglect myself. Use this week to restore, refocus, and refill me. I will use what you give me for your glory!

In The Name of Jesus, Amen.

WEEK 10: Help Me Handle It When I Need a Refill!

Day 2

BE CAREFUL WHERE YOU GET YOUR REFILL FROM!

Today's Passage
And be not drunk with wine, wherein is excess; but be filled with the Spirit; (Eph. 5:18).

Today's Point to Practice
The worst thing you can do to a beautiful automobile is put cheap gas in it. It will cause it to sputter, jerk, and run horribly. We live in the age of the cyber church. This means that people pick up sermons, notes, and even Bible lessons on the World Wide Web. This may prove to be convenient, but it is certainly not safe! Everyone with the Bible is not called to handle God's word. Like bad gasoline, it causes believers to stumble, fail, and falter along the way.

A few years ago, I purchased some gasoline from a station that appeared to be a foxhole. My better judgment told me not to do it. However, I did not listen. The result was internal mechanical problems because the gas I purchased was not good. When Paul urges the church at Ephesus not to be drunk with wine, he is really saying, be careful what you put in that temple of yours! Too much wine and not enough of God's Word can get you in trouble.

The best place to get a refill is from a "called" servant of the most High God who has studied God's Word and will proclaim it with passion, truth, accuracy, and integrity!

Today's Push
Stop believing every Internet preacher you hear. Some refills will cost you more than you will bargain for. Get a Bible and study it with someone skilled and trained to tell you what it means.

READ - 2 Timothy 2:15

Today's Prayer
Eternal God, our Father, I humbly ask you to fill my life with your Word and heal me with what you have said from your throne. Please, O God, order my steps in your Word.

In The Name of Jesus, Amen.

WEEK 10: Help Me Handle It When I Need a Refill!

Day 3

IF YOU REALLY NEED A REFILL LEARN TO PARTNER WITH THE RIGHT PEOPLE!

Today's Passage
And be not drunk with wine, wherein is excess; but be filled with the Spirit; (Eph. 5:18).

Today's Point To Practice
Did you know that the people you partner with define who you are? Are you aware that some people drain you of your joy, peace, and strength? When you need to be refilled and restored, you must be near the right people!

When Paul tells the church in Ephesus to be filled with the Spirit, he is saying to get near God and God's people. Remember this: the Holy Spirit is the sweetest person on Earth. He dwells with us, He seals us, and He teaches us. He empowers us, He enlightens us, and He strengthens us! His Spirit dwells within the hearts of those who, by faith, believe in Jesus Christ! If you want to be filled with the Spirit, you need to be near believers who love the Lord and are filled with the presence of God.

Interestingly, people can damage your life or do great good. Those who do damage often leave scars, bruises, and unwarranted hurt. However, those who do good bless you, help you, and improve your life. An old saying suggests you can do bad all by yourself! Make sure that the people in your life love God and are filled with His Spirit.

Today's Push
Mean, negative, evil, envious, jealous, shady, messy, indiscriminate people are those people that you should run from. Run to and partner with people who are so in love with the Lord that His love causes them to love you.

READ - St. John 14:34-35

Today's Prayer
Merciful Master, my prayer today for the life you have given me is this: please put the right people in my life.

In The Name of Jesus, Amen.

WEEK 10: Help Me Handle It When I Need a Refill!

Day 4

WHAT YOU REALLY NEED IS ANOTHER DOSE OF THE HOLY GHOST!

Today's Passage
And be not drunk with wine, wherein is excess; but be filled with the Spirit; (Eph. 5:18).

Today's Point To Practice
As believers in Jesus Christ, we believe in the Godhead. This is a reference to the Trinity or how we see God. We believe God is a Father with a plan for our lives and has adopted us by faith into His magnificent family (Eph. 1:4-6). We believe in the Son, Jesus Christ, who died on the cross to pay the price for our sins (Eph. 1:7-12). And we believe in the Holy Spirit. The purpose of the Holy Spirit given to us in the Scriptures is to do two primary things. First of all, He seals us until the day of redemption. This seal is once and for all. It is never removed. Once you hear the gospel and believe it by faith, you are sealed at that moment with the Holy Spirit (Eph. 1:13-14).

With this in mind, it is essential to embrace the fact that the Holy Spirit not only seals those who believe but also fills us with His presence. It is imperative to note that no believer in Christ is always filled with the Spirit. One day, a young seminary student asked Dr. Dwight L Moody if he was filled with the Spirit. Dr. Moody replied, "Yes, I am filled with the spirit, but I keep my life under His gracious faucet because I leak occasionally."

In other words, what Dr. Moody said was this: Every now and then I need another dose of the Holy Ghost. When Paul presents this argument to the Ephesian Church regarding the Holy Spirit, he teaches them an ageless truth. One that says the only way to stay filled with the Spirit is to keep asking Him for a refill.

Today's Push
Never forget this, and hold onto it for the rest of your time on Earth: it's OK to ask God for more of Him. We spend a lot of time asking the Lord for things from Him. However, there are times when what you need is simply more of Him! READ - Proverbs 8:17

Today's Prayer
Lord, my soul thirsts for you, and my heart yearns for your presence. Fill me with who you are so I can love and live like you did when you walked the Earth.

In The Name of Jesus, Amen.

WEEK 10: Help Me Handle It When I Need a Refill!

Day 5

WHEN YOU'RE FULL YOU OPERATE MUCH BETTER!

Today's Passage
And be not drunk with wine, wherein is excess; but be filled with the Spirit; (Eph. 5:18).

Today's Point To Practice
An automobile is made with an engine part called a fuel injector. When petroleum in the gas tank runs low, the fuel injector aims to protect the engine from picking up trash that could harm the automobile. With this in mind, most engines are highly acceptable to damage when they are low on fuel: the trash that is sometimes found in gasoline rests at the bottom of the gas tank. Therefore, when the tank is empty, a car can sputter, pop, jerk, and even turn completely off.

Your Spirit is the engine that fuels everything in your life. And when you are low on the fuel you need to progress forward, sometimes we malfunction. To prevent this, believers in Christ should do what Paul admonishes the church in Ephesus to do. He says, "....be filled with the spirit…"

When you are full, you play better, serve better, and have a better perspective. This is why being filled with the Spirit is so important. When you are filled with God's Spirit you are able to faithfully function at your best.

Today's Push
Living by faith is always easier when you are filled with the Holy Spirit and walking according to His Word. To do otherwise is not wise.

READ - Romans 5:5

Today's Prayer
God of grace and Lord of glory, I'm stronger and function better in faith when I'm closer to you. I find strength in your Love, peace in your presence, and hope in your touch. If you're not too busy right now, please touch me. Fill me with your Spirit Lord and Thank you for always being present for me.

In The Name of Jesus, Amen.

WEEK 10: Help Me Handle It When I Need a Refill!

Day 6

BEING EMPTY IS NOT FUNNY, IT'S DANGEROUS!

Today's Passage
And be not drunk with wine, wherein is excess; but be filled with the Spirit; (Eph. 5:18).

Today's Point To Practice
The I-10 is the most extended freeway system in the nation and runs through the heart of the city of Beaumont, Texas, like a crimson cord through a white quilt. The problem with it, however, is that there is always some type of delay on it. If it's not a construction delay, it's a traffic accident. And, if it's not a traffic accident, there's some debris in the road that everyone is trying to avoid. And, if it's not some debris in the road, a trucker has fallen asleep and crashed in the middle of the freeway. In short, it's always a mess.

One day, while headed westbound on the I-10, things were moving smoothly when, suddenly, things came to a screeching halt. Nothing was moving at all. After things started to move, I eventually discovered the source of the delay. It was something I did not expect to see. I pulled slowly past a parked car in the middle of the freeway with the driver standing in front of it with a gas can in his hand. It was a guy who was out of gas. You see, he went past E and passed the red marking on the gas gauge to a place called empty. He had nothing else in the tank! People in the other westbound vehicles were laughing at him. But it was not funny to me; it was dangerous. He put himself in danger, and he endangered the lives of countless others on I-10 just because he was empty. The Apostle Paul's words in the passage not only speak truth to us because he instructs us to "...be filled with the spirit..." but they bless us antithetically because when we are not filled with the Spirit, the consequences can be harmful. They can produce mishaps, slip-ups, mess-ups, disobedience, lawlessness, and even outright rebellion.

Today's Push
Do not get caught living empty when the Lord offers free refills. Never forget this: just because you are empty does not mean you have to stay in that condition. READ - Acts 2:4

Today's Prayer
Lord Jesus, I have had moments, times, and seasons when I was empty and knew it. I made mistakes that I could have avoided and I had times when I could have made better decisions. Please fill me with your Spirit and show me your presence. Thank you for loving me unconditionally.

In The Name of Jesus, Amen.

WEEK 10: Help Me Handle It When I Need a Refill!

Day 7

FILL-UP'S ARE FREE BECAUSE THEY'VE ALREADY BEEN PAID FOR!

Today's Passage
And be not drunk with wine, wherein is excess; but be filled with the Spirit; (Eph. 5:18).

Today's Point To Practice
My mother would wait until her car was beyond E, burning fumes, and nearly had nothing left before she pulled into the Gulf Station near the Astrodome for a refill. Mr. Ben, the station owner, would walk up to my mother's driver's side window and ask what she needed, and mother would say, "I need a refill; fill it up." Mr. Ben would then retreat to the pump, and something unique would happen. Her gas needle would shift slowly from E (empty) to F (full). She would instruct us to raise the windows, and she would turn on the air conditionering and the radio.

After the tank was filled, Mr. Ben returned to the car, and my mother would say, "How much do I owe you?" He would reply, "Fill-ups are free because they have already been paid for!" You see, my Father had already paid Mr. Ben, so when it was time for him to collect, there was no debt owed or bill to be paid.

Just like my earthly Father had already paid for my mother's fill-ups, our Heavenly Father has paid for our spiritual refills through the death of His only begotten Son, Jesus Christ on the cross.

Today's Push
It makes no sense to remain spiritually empty when God has made provisions for you to stay filled, fueled, and faithful at no cost. When you are trying to handle being empty, go to the Lord in prayer and ask Him to fill you until you want no more.

READ - St. Luke 11:13

Today's Prayer
O Lord, today is the day that my spiritual emptiness ends. Never again will I allow my life to be in such a condition. I realize that your death at the cross was my total payment for everything that I would ever need from you. Thank you for being such a good, kind, and gracious God.

In The Name of Jesus, Amen.

WEEK 11: Help Me Handle This Mess I'm In

Day 1

SOMETIMES I HATE THE SHAPE THAT I'M IN, BUT I LOVE THE HOPE THAT I HAVE!

Our Passage of Study
And the LORD God called unto Adam, and said unto him, Where art thou? And he said, I heard thy voice in the Garden, and I was afraid, because I was naked; and I hid myself (Gen. 3:9-10).

Today's Parable
One thing is sure about the human condition: at some point in your sojourn on the planet, you will discover that your life is a mess and needs to be repaired. Have you ever had a point when things were a mess? It's that place where you work every day, but you find yourself trapped in financial ruin because you spend too much. It's that moment where you realize that your greatest enemy is in-a-me, and every time you attempt to fix yourself, something else breaks. It's that time when familiar friends with bad habits recycle sinful spirits in your life, and they assist you with going back into stuff you just knew you had been delivered from. It's that occurrence where you know right from wrong, but wrong makes you feel right and is readily accessible.

To say it clearly, making a mess of things is easy. When I was about eleven years old, my Father invited me to work with him in the sugar cane fields of Louisiana. He didn't ask me; he told me to get dressed. We were going to Melville, and I obeyed because I did not want to face the consequences. Nonetheless, we arrive in the tiny town and are given instructions on what to keep and what to cut. There were several of us in the field, and I was determined to work hard and fast to get my work over so I could chew some of that cane, eat catfish caught from the river, fried extra crispy, of course, and play.

The workload was given, and the rules were explained. I outworked everyone, and by the time we took our first break, I was over halfway finished. I was so proud of myself until I heard my Father shout, "Who in the world cut these rows over here!" Everyone pointed at me, laughing uncontrollably. My dad said, "This thing is a mess, and you have ruined all of this cane!" You see, I was in bad shape, but my only hope was that my Father would not kill me for the horrible mess that I had made.

It was my first mess, but it was certainly not my last. Here's a great devotional question: Have you ever made a mess you could not reverse or undo? Have you ever worked hard to do it right, and things still came out wrong? Have you ever looked at your life and looked towards heaven and prayed, "Lord, help me with this mess I'm in?"

WEEK 11: Help Me Handle This Mess I'm In

This week, we will intently study Adam's mess in the Garden of Eden and how the Lord of Heaven helped him handle it. The shout of the day is this: God never gave up on Adam, and He will never give up on you.

Today's Prayer

Heavenly Father, I approach you right now knowing that parts of my life are a mess. I'm not perfect, and that's why I need you more now than ever before. Thank you for never changing your mind about me. Heal me and help me is my sincere supplication, plea, prayer, and petition.

In The Name of Jesus, Amen.

WEEK 11: Help Me Handle This Mess I'm In

Day 2

HE KNOWS YOUR SIN, BUT HE CALLS YOU BY YOUR NAME!

Today's Passage
And the LORD God called unto Adam, and said unto him, Where art thou? And he said, I heard thy voice in the Garden, and I was afraid, because I was naked; and I hid myself (Gen. 3:9-10).

Today's Point To Practice
People love to gossip and discuss the sins and faults of others while at the same time ignoring the faults and failures they have for themselves. It's why social media is so loaded. People stalk your page and the pages of others, looking for a mess to talk about so that they can discuss your faults, failures, mishaps, mess-ups, and misfortunes. We live in a generation of finger-pointing, name-calling, flawed people who find great pleasure in highlighting your sins and calling them out by name.

The blessing in today's lesson is that God is not like people in this stead because He knows your sins but calls you by your name. In the passage listed above, the Lord comes walking in the cool of the day to fellowship with the man He had made, Adam. God left Adam in the Garden to keep it and have dominion over everything created. However, upon His arrival, Adam was found hiding behind some bushes because he had made a complete mess of things.

The healing virtue in this passage is that God does not say, "Hey, you backstabbing, no good for nothing, liar you." The passage reads, "And the Lord God called unto Adam...."

Today's Push
For God to call Adam by his name was huge! It meant that He did not see Adam for the mistake that He had made, even though He made the mistake. At this point, you should be rejoicing, and here is why: God knows your mistakes, too. However, instead of referring to you as any of them, He calls you by your name. READ - Isaiah 43:1

Today's Prayer
Thank you, Jesus, for remembering my name and not calling me the titles of the sins I have committed. Bless your name, O God, for being gracious and kind to me. I'm forever indebted to you for the rest of my life.

In The Name of Jesus, Amen.

WEEK 11: Help Me Handle This Mess I'm In

Day 3

YOU ARE NOT THE MESS YOU HAVE MADE!

Today's Passage
And the LORD God called unto Adam, and said unto him, Where art thou? And he said, I heard thy voice in the Garden, and I was afraid, because I was naked; and I hid myself (Gen. 3:9-10).

Today's Point To Practice
I have been blessed with two of the most wonderful children in the world: Sumone and Jonathan. When Sumone was about three or four years old, she decided to surprise us with her artistic abilities. Our family had just moved into a new home, and Sumone had a room for herself. My daughter retreated to her room and was extremely quiet. I just knew she was asleep. However, such was certainly not the case. Sister girl was in there doing the most! She had taken the Crayons that we bought her and transformed the walls of her room into a decorative canvas. If you can catch my drift, it was a painting with a twist.

She invited my wife and me into her room only to discover that parts of our white walls had been colored. Here's the news you want to hear: even though she created a total mess, she was not the mess she had made. She was our Baby, not our mess. She was our little girl, not a mishap that took place. She was just as much our child with colored walls as when the walls were white.

Today's Push
Sometimes, you look at the mistakes you have made in your life and feel like you are the mistakes you have made. But nothing could be further from the truth. You are not the sins you have committed, you are not the errors of your way, and you are not the misfortunes you have caused. You are the Lord's child, no matter what.

READ - 1 John 1:9-10

Today's Prayer
God of glory and Christ of the cross, I call upon you right now to look beyond my faults and see my needs. I need your forgiveness, guidance, and presence within me to become so much like you that I learn to please you.

In The Name of Jesus, Amen.

WEEK 11: Help Me Handle This Mess I'm In

Day 4

WHY ARE YOU WHERE YOU ARE?

Today's Passage
And the LORD God called unto Adam, and said unto him, Where art thou? And he said, I heard thy voice in the Garden, and I was afraid, because I was naked; and I hid myself (Gen. 3:9-10).

Today's Point To Practice
When you read the two verses printed above, notice that the Lord calls Adam by his name and then asks him, "Where are you?" Think about this query for a moment. If the Lord God is the one that is asking the question and He is God, He already knows where Adam is located. After all, God knows everything because He is omniscient. So then, since God knows everything, this question is not about Adams's location but rather his disposition. With this in mind, it should be stated, "Adam, why are you where you are?" Here's the idea in the text: the Lord left Adam in charge of everything, but when He returned, He found him hiding behind bushes and being afraid.

Take a moment and consider this question, which is one God asked of the humans He created. Now aim this query at your life and honestly answer it: Why are you where you are? Why are you in the condition that you are in? Why are you not living up to your potential? Why are you not where the Lord wants you? How did you end up being where you are?

Today's Push
Remember that where you are now is not your final destination. It is, however, a point in your pilgrimage on the planet that you must consider where you are headed from here.

It does not matter how old or young you are. What is most important is what you do with the remaining time. And that should begin with an honest assessment of this one question: "Why are you where you are?" READ - Psalms 31:4

Today's Prayer
Lord Jesus, I know where I am, and you are not finished with my life. As I pray this petition to you, I sincerely desire you to use my life for your glory and guide me like never before. I belong to you. My life is in your hands, so mold me like you are my potter. Shape me, recreate me, and use me for your glory.

In The Name of Jesus, Amen.

WEEK 11: Help Me Handle This Mess I'm In

Day 5

HE'S GOT A MASTER PLAN!

Today's Passage
And the LORD God called unto Adam, and said unto him, Where art thou? And he said, I heard thy voice in the Garden, and I was afraid, because I was naked; and I hid myself (Gen. 3:9-10).

Today's Point To Practice
The Bible is a record of the divine-human encounter. It records how God has dealt with all of humankind in times past so that we can embrace how the God of human history deals with us today. With this in mind, re-read our passage of study for the week just once more. Notice this: when the Lord returns to find Adam in the Garden, he is in the worst condition ever. He has done precisely what God has told him not to do. He has failed miserably. He has gone from handling his business by faith to hiding in fear behind bushes. The scene is a total catastrophe. It would have been an excellent time to start over. To get rid of both Adam and Eve by letting them die off and then start all over with a new man and woman. But this is not what the Lord does at all.

At this point in human history, we can see the commencement of a Master Plan. God does not trash the people. He does not beat them, thrash them, or torment them at all. He keeps them! He knows what they have done, is aware of their disobedience, and is conscious of how they have failed. Yet, the good news reported from the Garden is that there is no news of God giving up on the people He created. We have a God who seems concerned with three things: why are they where they are, who have they been listening to, and have they done the wrong thing? This is just the beginning of the Master plan that our Master pushes and presses, highlighting the onset of how amazing His grace will really be for us after the cross in the future.

Today's Push
READ - Romans 5:20-21

Today's Prayer
Lord, there have been times when I was just like Adam. I did precisely what you commanded me not to do. For Adam, it was only forbidden fruit, but for me, it has been too many mistakes for me to recount. However, just like you decided to keep them, you have kept me for some reason. O God, may your plans for my life reign forever and ever. Grace is what I need, even though I know I do not deserve it.

In The Name of Jesus, Amen.

WEEK 11: Help Me Handle This Mess I'm In

Day 6

HE COVERS YOU SO THAT HE CAN REDEEM YOU!

Today's Passage
And the LORD God called unto Adam, and said unto him, Where art thou? And he said, I heard thy voice in the Garden, and I was afraid, because I was naked; and I hid myself (Gen. 3:10).

Today's Point To Practice
When Adam and Eve realize they are naked, they do their best to cover themselves. The narrative recorded in Genesis 3 says that they sewed fig leaves together to cover their nudity. Please know this is the first official cover-up story we have encountered in human history. Based on this report, there needed to be more leaves to cover everything, so human efforts to cover up personal inadequacy proved from the onset to be insufficient.

So here is what the Lord did for them: He sacrificed an animal, took animal skins, and covered their nakedness. Can you see the redemptive portrait yet? God provided a sacrifice that included blood; He then used the skin of the animal to provide cover for the people that He would keep!

This is a solid picture of redemption that should cause you to rejoice!

Today's Push
Remember this one emphatic truth: there are only two types of people in the world: covered and uncovered. If you are covered, it means that you have accepted the finished work of Jesus Christ on the cross, and you believe that He has risen as the scriptures teach and will reign forever as our King! If you are uncovered, you are still trying to stitch together leaves to find a way to cover your faults, failures, and sins.

READ - Ephesians 1:7

Today's Prayer
Jesus, it is because of your blood that I am covered. It is purely because of your sacrifice made for me that I have been made righteous in your sight. Thank you for loving me enough to die in my place. It is my sincere petition to serve you until the day I die.

In The Name of Jesus, Amen.

WEEK 11: Help Me Handle This Mess I'm In

Day 7

WHAT YOU DON'T HAVE GRACE WILL PROVIDE!

Today's Passage
And the LORD God called unto Adam, and said unto him, Where art thou? And he said, I heard thy voice in the Garden, and I was afraid, because I was naked; and I hid myself (Gen. 3:9-10).

Today's Point To Practice
On day one of this week, I shared the story of how my Father had me working in the sugarcane fields of Louisiana, and I made a mess of things. Do you remember that? I had cut off the parts of the sugarcane that I was supposed to keep. My cousins were laughing uncontrollably. To make matters worse, I was to keep a portion of the sugarcane to chew for myself as a reward for working so hard in the field that day. It was a mess, and I was embarrassed. I wanted to crawl under a rock and hide myself forever. And, to add insult to injury, I had disappointed my dad, who gave everyone specific instructions on what to keep and cut.

Well, we are leaving the field for the day, and we have gathered around the bed of this old Chevy pickup to get our portion of the cane to keep. My cousins were chuckling and grinning because I would not have any sugarcane; after all, I was the one who cut it wrong. I'm the one who did exactly what I was not supposed to do. As they were handing out sugarcane, my dad did the unthinkable. He said, "And last but not least, Bobby, I have some sugarcane for you too. I want you to have my cane because you never quit trying, and you never stopped working even though you made some mistakes. You worked until the end of the day. So I know you don't have sugarcane in your sack, but I want to give you mine!"

Today's Push
Can you see grace written all over this story? What my Father did for me is the same thing God did for Adam and Eve in the Garden. They deserved nothing, but God gave them what they did not deserve. Grace is God's unmerited favor given to us and never earned. READ - Ephesians 2:8-9

Today's Prayer
Lord, receiving your grace makes me want to serve you even more. I feel privileged to be the recipient of your goodness, and I am compelled to live for you daily. I know that I'm not perfect, so I don't like the shape I'm in, but because I'm in Christ Jesus, I love the hope I have.

In The Name of Jesus, Amen.

WEEK 12: Help Me Handle My Losses

Day 1

IT'S A TEST, SO DON'T LET GOD DOWN!

Our Passage of Study
Then Job arose, and rent his mantle, and shaved his head, and fell down upon the ground, and worshipped, And said, Naked came I out of my mother's womb, and naked shall I return thither: the LORD gave, and the LORD hath taken away; blessed be the name of the LORD (Job 1:20-21, KJV).

Today's Parable
The hurricane season for the year 2024 presented a duo of storms that battered the Floridian coast. Hurricane Helene came ashore near Tallahassee as a category three storm, causing damage as far as the eye could see. And, just a few weeks later, Hurricane Milton pounded the same coastline with a category-five storm. A hurricane can't get any larger than that. Milton left seventeen people dead, thousands without power, and millions affected by wind and water damage. The entire region was declared a national disaster.

Amber Henry rode the storm out in her Lakeland, Florida home. The transformer exploded, and flood water came rushing through the windows of her house, causing losses beyond her imagination. One family that appeared on CNN highlighted the story of a man standing outside of his home with what seemed to be a Bible in his hand. The wreckage behind looked as if his house had imploded and was utterly destroyed. In a media-like fashion, the reporter asked him what he would do now, and his reply truly blessed me. He said, "I'm going to keep trusting the Lord." The young reporter said, "But, you have lost everything," but he offered a statement that was so rooted in faith there was no follow-up. He said, "Ma'am, God gave me my house and cars. My family is safe, and that's what matters most, and He gave me them too. This is a test! I will not complain, and I will not let God down!"

Believers go through periods of suffering for several different reasons. However, they can all be categorized by placing human suffering into two lanes. On the one hand, we suffer for the sake of discipline. God loves His children so much that He refuses to let them live in continued disobedience, so from time to time, He disciplines us (Hebrews 12:6-11). On the other hand, we suffer for the cause of blessing. The most excellent form of blessing is where God places your life on the witness stand of human hurt and loss and then allows satan to cross-examine the witness. During satan's permitted attacks, God depends on us to stand firm in the face of loss, hurt, and calamity and say what Job said during his testing time. Job said, "The Lord giveth and the Lord hath taken away; blessed be the name of the Lord."

WEEK 12: Help Me Handle My Losses

Studying the verses above will empower and encourage you for the next several days. What we learn from these scriptures will change your life forever, as you will be empowered to handle life when, as a Christian, you go through seasons of loss. After all, it's only a test, and you can't afford to let God down!

Today's Prayer
Unto thee O God do I place my trust. Thankfully and joyfully, I have come into your presence, and today, I ask you for the faith of Job to help me face and deal with my losses. If you could help him, you can do the same for me.

In The Name of Jesus, Amen.

WEEK 12: Help Me Handle My Losses

Day 2

REMEMBER THAT YOU AND EVERYTHING YOU OWN IS GOD'S PROPERTY!

Today's Passage
Then Job arose, and rent his mantle, and shaved his head, and fell down upon the ground, and worshipped, And said, Naked came I out of my mother's womb, and naked shall I return thither: the LORD gave, and the LORD hath taken away; blessed be the name of the LORD (Job 1:20-21, KJV).

Today's Point To Practice
Often, when people face losses of any sort, we are quick to speak of what has been taken from us as if it were ours. My Father, my mother, my son, my daughter, my health, my house, my car, my….my…my. We speak of both people and things as if they are exclusively ours. But nothing could be further from the truth. With this in mind, we live with a closed hand. And, when the Lord has to take something from us, He often has to break our hand to get it out. In today's lesson narrative, Job goes through a battery of severe losses. He loses all ten of his children, their homes, his livestock, camels, sheep, and horses. His wife even tells him to curse God and die. However, Job decides to do otherwise. He says, "…Naked came I out of my mother's womb, and naked shall I return thither: the LORD gave, and the LORD hath taken away; blessed be the name of the LORD." Here's what Job understood that we, too, should internalize. There is a difference between stewardship and ownership. God is the only owner of what belongs on the Earth. Scripture says, "The Earth is the Lords.…" (Psalms 24a). In short, the Deed of Imminent Domain suggests God owns everything here. With this in mind, we are stewards. We own nothing, and upon our passing from this place, we must give it all back.

Today's Push
As a believer in Jesus Christ, you are a steward, not an owner. God holds the deed to your life in the hallow of His mighty hand! With this in mind, nothing on earth belongs to you: not your family, not your friends, your resources, your property, or anything that exists on earth.

READ - Psalms 24

Today's Prayer
Lord of creation, forgive me for thinking that what I lost was mine when it was yours the entire time. I, too, belong to you, Lord Jesus, and you have always taken great care of me. I bless your name for the stewardship you have entrusted to me.

In The Name of Jesus, Amen.

WEEK 12: Help Me Handle My Losses

Day 3

REALIZE THAT GOD'S GOODNESS IS YOUR POSSESSION!

Today's Passage
Then Job arose, and rent his mantle, and shaved his head, and fell down upon the ground, and worshipped, And said, Naked came I out of my mother's womb, and naked shall I return thither: the LORD gave, and the LORD hath taken away; blessed be the name of the LORD (Job 1:20-21, KJV).

Today's Point To Practice
Have you ever faced a time of severe loss in your life? If you can say yes, take a moment and think back to that time. Try your best to remember your tears and your sense of human hurt. Are you there yet? Try to recall what it felt like when you first heard the news. Now, ask yourself this one question: How did you make it through this season of your life without losing your mind, trashing your faith, and giving up on God? The answer is simple: the Lord held you and kept you.

This is what makes the Lord so good. It is why Job is still sound in mind and body in the above story and why you did not fall completely apart. God was with you the entire time. When you look in retrospect at the season of your life that was most difficult, here is what you have to conclude: He was there to wipe your tears. He was there to hold your hand. And, if you were too weak to hold His hand, God picked you up and carried you through.

He is, without a shadow of a doubt, a good God! He is good enough to wipe your tears, lift your head, and strengthen you from the inside out so that you can endure from the outside in.

Today's Push
The goodness of God is seen most clearly not when He keeps us from seasons of difficulty but when He sustains us with His power while we endure them. READ - Psalms 145:9

Today's Prayer
Eternal God, my Father, I bow my head before you. Thank you for being so good to me. I realize that even in the darkest times of my life, you were still good to me. Forgive me for complaining. I have been guilty of that. And please pardon my lack of gratitude. Today, I praise your name for the goodness you blessed me with when my losses were ever-present.

In The Name of Jesus, Amen.

WEEK 12: Help Me Handle My Losses

Day 4

IT'S NOT JUST WHAT HE TOOK, IT'S WHAT HE LET YOU KEEP!

Today's Passage
Then Job arose, and rent his mantle, and shaved his head, and fell down upon the ground, and worshipped, And said, Naked came I out of my mother's womb, and naked shall I return thither: the LORD gave, and the LORD hath taken away; blessed be the name of the LORD (Job 1:20-21, KJV).

Today's Point To Practice
My older brother James Adolph was murdered in August of 1980 on East Mount Houston Road in Houston, Texas. It was a traumatic moment for our family. There was hurt, tears, anger, resentment, blame, disbelief, and prayers; all balled up into one huge package called grief. My mother just stared at the walls of her room and screamed from time to time. My sister walked through the house just crying uncontrollably. My younger brother Ron and I were too young to comprehend what occurred entirely. And my Father was silent and speechless. Death had found our home. Not just death but murder. A mystery that to this day has gone unsolved. My oldest brother Sonny was the one who took the cake and upset our family's proverbial apple cart. During the recession at my brother's funeral, as we walked out of the cathedral of Little Union Baptist Church in Settegast, he leaped and shouted thank you, Jesus! You have been so good to us! I thought he had lost his mind until I asked him why he would shout such praise at a time like that. Sonny's faith blessed me! He said, "Bobby, it's not what He just took; it's what He let us keep! He took Butch, but He let us keep everybody else!" One thing that will help you endure the loss of anything is to remember that God always leaves more than He takes. Learn the value of not taking the people you love for granted. Treasure them while you have them. Their presence is a gift from the Lord to you.

Today's Push
God could take everyone from you just like He did in the story of Job. But, in most cases, He has allowed you to keep more than He has ever taken. Live every day like what you have could be taken from you because it belongs to God. And, if the Lord left you something to keep, learn to be thankful for what you have. READ - Psalms 100:5

Today's Prayer
Thank you, Jesus, for the people and the things you have allowed me to keep in my life. Help me treat them like they are a chosen treasure because I realize they could be gone. Your grace speaks to my soul each time I look at all you have left with me, which blesses me. O God, thank you again.

In The Name of Jesus, Amen.

WEEK 12: Help Me Handle My Losses

Day 5

LET GO AND HOLD ON!

Today's Passage

Then Job arose, and rent his mantle, and shaved his head, and fell down upon the ground, and worshipped, And said, Naked came I out of my mother's womb, and naked shall I return thither: the LORD gave, and the LORD hath taken away; blessed be the name of the LORD (Job 1:20-21, KJV).

Today's Point To Practice

How did Job survive it all? The secret to Job's survival is hidden within the confines of the text. Job knows what it takes to survive death in the family, loss of property, loss of income, loss of a spouse, and a group of bad advice-giving "so-called" friends. Job knows how to cope, conquer, and overcome. What does Job know, you ask? Here it is, and always remember it. Job understood the paradox of personal progress. Here is the paradox: let go and hold on. Wait a moment; how can you let go and hold simultaneously? It's like saying, "Come see my jumbo shrimp" or "Come see my new antiques." To let go and hold on does not make sense at first glance, but it makes perfect sense if you look at it by faith.

If you will endure the stormy weather that life sometimes throws your way with our Lord's permission, you must know when to let go. By this, I mean let go of the people, things, and losses God has taken from you. If it's gone, it's gone. However, learn the value of holding on. Hold on to the Lord's hand. Hold on to your memory of what once was. Hold on to the joy that you have. Hold on to the portion that He provides. And, hold on to the promises of our Prince of Peace who declares, "....and lo I am with you always even to the end of the age" (St. Matthew 28:20).

Today's Push

The believer who will always endure difficult times is the saint who knows how to let go and when to hold on! READ - Isaiah 41:13

Today's Prayer

Gracious and everlasting God, give me the power to let go. There are times I hold on, and it kills me. Please help me accept your will, knowing that my losses are always in your hands. And, Lord, give me the strength and power to hold on. God, if I ever become too weak to hold on to you at that moment, please hold on to me and do not let me go.

In The Name of Jesus, Amen.

WEEK 12: Help Me Handle My Losses

Day 6

THEIR ABSENCE HURT, BUT HIS PRESENCE HEALS!

Today's Passage
Then Job arose, and rent his mantle, and shaved his head, and fell down upon the ground, and worshipped, And said, Naked came I out of my mother's womb, and naked shall I return thither: the LORD gave, and the LORD hath taken away; blessed be the name of the LORD (Job 1:20-21, KJV).

Today's Point To Practice
OK, for total transparency, I want to be clear that loss hurts. PERIOD! Not long ago, I spoke with a member of our congregation whose mother lived to be 103 years old. The family made a request for me to visit after their matriarch passed away and I readily acquiesced. When I arrived at their home to whisper words of prayer with them, the mood in the house was so heavy. It is not what I expected at all. After all, to live 103 years is a gift from the Lord, right? I thought they should have been joyful, happy, relieved, and in good spirits. However, I found something else. I walked into a house filled with tears, hurt, and boxes of tissue everywhere as children, grandchildren, family, and friends gathered to say goodbye.

One of her oldest daughters, who attends the Antioch Church, whispered in my ear, "I'm glad you are here to pray for us, Pastor. This entire family is taking the loss of my mother very hard. We know we were blessed to have her all of our lives. But she's gone right now, and it still hurts." It was then that I realized that the absence of a loved one hurts no matter how old or young they may be when they pass away.

The great thing about the Lord, however, is this: in the absence of a loved one is the presence of God, and when you have more of His presence, you can certainly handle their absence.

Today's Push
In the presence of the Lord, there is always healing and wholeness. God is a healer; wherever He is everything will be alright. READ - St. Matthew 4:23-25

Today's Prayer
God, I have always known you to be a healer. If you are still in the healing business, please take my hurt and heal me. Thank you for healing and restoring me. I humbly ask that you always keep your hand on my life. This is my sincere supplication.

In The Name of Jesus, Amen.

WEEK 12: Help Me Handle My Losses

Day 7

GOD'S PRAISE IS YOUR PURPOSE

Today's Passage
Then Job arose, and rent his mantle, and shaved his head, and fell down upon the ground, and worshipped, And said, Naked came I out of my mother's womb, and naked shall I return thither: the LORD gave, and the LORD hath taken away; blessed be the name of the LORD (Job 1:20-21, KJV).

Today's Point To Practice
We have reached the end of a week of studying just one small passage of scripture. For the last few days, we have pulled and perused the confines of Job 1:20-21. The best news in the world we can lift from the passage is that the Lord is on both sides of the equation. Notice the text reads like this: "....the Lord giveth.....the Lord taketh..." Giving and taking are singular subjects, but the Lord is the grand object. With this in mind, you can handle your losses because the same God is involved in both the giving and taking you encounter in life. If you can trust God while He is giving, you can trust God while He is taking.

Notice how this pericope concludes. Job says, "Blessed be the name of the Lord!" This moment of human loss ends with praise for the Lord He loves and serves.

You see, God's praise is your purpose. Anyone can shout thank you when all is well. But, it takes great faith to shout thank you when your heart is heavy, and your burdens are real.

Today's Push
The gentleman from Florida who had just been hit by Hurricanes Helene and Milton said it best: " This is a test, and I will not let God down!" The best way not to let Him down is to lift Him up. Praise is what we do!

READ - Psalms 34:1

Today's Prayer
Lord, I have had my share of losses. When I look back at how you kept me, sustained me, and delivered me, my soul shouts with joy: Worthy is the Lamb of God! Thank you, Jesus, because it would have been too much for me to handle without you. But because you were there, I can celebrate the fact that I made it.

In The Name of Jesus, Amen.

WEEK 13: Help Me Handle Satanic Attacks Launched Against Me

Day 1

GOD IS STILL IN CONTROL!

Our Passage of Study
And the Lord said, Simon, Simon, behold, satan hath desired to have you, that he may sift you as wheat: But I have prayed for thee, that thy faith fail not: and when thou art converted, strengthen thy brethren (St. Luke 22:31-32).

Today's Parable
If you are a believer in Jesus Christ, you can be sure of two things: Jesus is Lord, and satan is going to attack you. Our enemy is sneaky, sly, slick, and subtle. He is tricky and treacherous and is an expert at setting traps for those of us who love God. He is a deceiver. He is the greatest liar known to humankind. He is described in the scriptures as a serpent, a thief, and the accuser of the brethren. Jesus says that his agenda is to "... kill, steal and destroy...." (St. John 10:10b). He is dangerous.

I will never forget the first satanic attack I had ever witnessed. It took place in Little Zion Baptist Church during what appeared to be a typical Sunday evening service. My oldest sibling, Sonny, was the Pastor of a growing congregation of believers in Houston's northeast sector.

There was a woman within our congregation whose name was Flossy. She was caring, vibrant, beautiful, and extremely friendly. She started in a discipleship class for women, but she grew so fast that she became a teacher and a servant leader of the church.

Flossy was sitting on her normal pew one Sunday night, but she was cold, distant, and removed, not her usual self. Minister Ward, a small Holy Ghost-filled preacher, said, "Sister Flossy, are you okay?" And she did not respond. He stepped down from the pulpit and said, "The Lord is leading me to pray for you." As Minister Ward approached her, she sat extremely still, and when he touched her, he started to pray. Flossy began to bark like an animal and respond with crazy gyrations and body motions, like one of a snake. Minister Ward took a step back and said, "Church, Sister Flossy is under satanic attack! Demons are trying to destroy her, and we will not stand for that."

The church went into prayer, and the Pastor and ministers started to pray for Sister Flossy. She collapsed like a dead person with foam rolling out of her mouth. When she regained consciousness, she stood up and did not remember a thing. Her face was all aglow, and her joy

WEEK 13: Help Me Handle Satanic Attacks Launched Against Me

was restored. Standing up, she asked, "What happened to me?" And the Pastor and Minister Ward told her that the enemy had her bound, but Christ had set her free!

This encounter taught me that the enemy attacks us when we least expect it. He sends temptation into our lives to cause subtle destruction, and he lies to us to get us off track and out of God's will.

Consider the above mentioned lesson, which presents our study passage for this week. Jesus warns His Disciple Peter that a satanic storm is on the horizon. The Lord tells Peter that the enemy seeks to sift him like wheat. However, the great news is that Satan's desire does not compare to our Lord's protection. Peter is informed that God is still on His side when the narrative concludes.

The purpose of this lesson is to remind believers that none of us are exempt from satan's tricks, traps, and treachery. The aim of this week's study is to arm every believer with Biblical truth regarding the ways of the enemy and the power of our advocate that we stand firm under any attack that God permits and concludes stronger than we have ever been.

Today's Prayer
God of deliverance, I pray right now, in the name of your Son and my Savior, that you give me the strength to stand against the enemy's methods and come out victorious. Keep your presence and power completely in control within me.

In The Name of Jesus, Amen.

WEEK 13: Help Me Handle Satanic Attacks Launched Against Me

Day 2

THE LORD COULD HAVE STOPPED IT BUT HE DIDN'T!

Today's Passage

And the Lord said, Simon, Simon, behold, Satan hath desired to have you, that he may sift you as wheat: But I have prayed for thee, that thy faith fail not: and when thou art converted, strengthen thy brethren (St. Luke 22:31-32).

Today's Point To Practice

To be forewarned is to be forearmed, right? After all, Jesus does warn Peter that satan is coming. The passage reads, ".....Simon, Simon behold satan hath desired to have you that he might sift you as wheat...." It should be noted that in Koine Greek (The common Greek language of the New Testament), there is no way to add an exclamation point to a word or phrase. So, the emphasis is placed on a grammatical construct to repeat it. So this passage reads with Jesus literally yelling at Peter, saying to him, "Simon! Satan is planning an attack against you!" To have the warning is great, right? But if the Lord knows that the attack is coming and He has all the power, why doesn't He stop it? Here's the truth observed from our lesson today: the Lord could have stopped it, but He didn't. And the question that looms ominously to be answered is why? Why doesn't the Lord stop the enemy from attacking us? Here's the answer, and never forget it: God allows satanic attacks because He wants to heighten your awareness of just how powerful His grace really is. In this way, God's grace strongly manifests itself when we are at our weakest point so that we might gain the strength needed from the Lord for the journey ahead. In short, the enemy meant it for your bad, but God allowed it for your good!

Today's Push

God does not stop satan from attacking us. He permits the attacks only to empower us with His grace so that what comes from the encounter is a stronger saint and a testimony that says, "....His grace is sufficient for me...." READ -2 Corinthians 12:5-12

Today's Prayer

Lord God of heaven, I have always known that you could have stopped the enemy from attacking me. But, right now, I know for myself that your grace is truly sufficient for me. Thank you for covering me, empowering me, and blessing me in the midst of what could have been satanic destruction.

In The Name of Jesus, Amen.

WEEK 13: Help Me Handle Satanic Attacks Launched Against Me

Day 3

IF THE DEVIL COULD HAVE IT HIS WAY, YOUR LIFE WOULD BE BROKEN INTO PIECES!

Today's Passage
And the Lord said, Simon, Simon, behold, Satan hath desired to have you, that he may sift you as wheat: But I have prayed for thee, that thy faith fail not: and when thou art converted, strengthen thy brethren (St. Luke 22:31-32).

Today's Point To Practice
The passage above says that satan wants to ".....sift you as wheat...." This agrarian talk refers to wheat and chaff being placed in a sifting device designed to separate the wheat from the chaff. Here's how it works: The grain is heavy, and the trash is light. Wheat and chaff are placed into a sifter, and because the wheat is heavier than the chaff, the wheat falls to the floor, and the chaff flies away.

By now, you should be thinking to yourself what in the world does this have to do with me while satan is trying to destroy me? There is a picture here that Jesus wants Peter to notice. You see, satan wants your life to look like the wheat and chaff that has been through the sifter. What does it look like? It seems like everything has been shredded to pieces!

My friend, this is what satan wants. He wants your life in pieces. The great news is that we serve a God who can take all of your pieces into His mighty hands and create a Masterpiece!

Today's Push
While satan wants your life in pieces, you have a Savior who wants you to have peace that goes beyond human comprehension, so be careful who you let hold your broken pieces. Only God knows what to do with them.

READ - Psalms 55:12

Today's Prayer
Today, O God, I am making a decision to bring my brokenness to you. The enemy has attacked me so many times, and each attack has left me in pieces. Lord, I give my broken pieces to you. Heal me, Lord, please.

In The Name of Jesus, Amen.

WEEK 13: Help Me Handle Satanic Attacks Launched Against Me

Day 4

HE'S TURNING IT AROUND JUST FOR YOU!

Today's Passage
And the Lord said, Simon, Simon, behold, Satan hath desired to have you, that he may sift you as wheat: But I have prayed for thee, that thy faith fail not: and when thou art converted, strengthen thy brethren (St. Luke 22:31-32).

Today's Point To Practice
How would you rejoice if today's word from the Lord was that He was turning it around for you? I cannot speak for you, but it fills my heart with gratitude. The passage of study listed above covers two verses. In verse 31, Satan is sifting us; however, verse 32 begins with the word "but." The term is used as a contrasting conjunction, suggesting that everything that came before it has been eliminated, deleted, and done away with.

In the 1970s, component sets were part of the music scene. People played 45s and albums—can you remember that? Now, when an album had completely finished one side, it would appear that all of the music was finished, but the DJ had a very important job at that point. His job was to take the album and flip it. And what appeared to be finished had more music to come.

Satan is mentioned in verse 31. But your Savior is declared in verse 32. In verse 31, the enemy tries to find a way to destroy you. But in verse 32, your advocate is fighting your battle so that you can come out on top no matter what. The best news in this passage is that our God allows the attack and then flips the script on the whole thing! The Lord of heaven does not allow what the enemy has planned to have the final word or the concluding matter in your life.

Today's Push
Do not panic when Satan seems to have your life in pieces. God has the power to flip it. The Lord you serve will turn everything around and make it work for your good! READ - Romans 8:28

Today's Prayer
Jesus, knowing that you are turning things around in my life causes me to hope only in you! I see the enemy is real, but my joy comes from knowing that my God is real, too, and He has no equal. O bless His holy and righteous name.

In The Name of Jesus, Amen.

WEEK 13: Help Me Handle Satanic Attacks Launched Against Me

Day 5

DON'T LET ANYTHING OR ANYBODY SEPARATE YOU FROM YOU!

Today's Passage
And the Lord said, Simon, Simon, behold, Satan hath desired to have you, that he may sift you as wheat: But I have prayed for thee, that thy faith fail not: and when thou art converted, strengthen thy brethren (St. Luke 22:31-32).

Today's Point To Practice
When hell breaks loose in your life, the enemy wants to isolate you to make you feel like no one else cares. Have you ever been there when you felt like you were all alone? Have you ever felt like no one cared? Have you ever felt like even God did not care about you? It is in moments like this that the enemy can be most deceitful. He whispers, "God let you down this time, didn't He?" The enemy will even say, "Where is that God of yours now?" The feeling of abandonment sets in, and satan convinces you to walk away from the Lord.

It is why passages like the one above are given to us in the scriptures. The Lord wants you to know that He never wants you separated from Him. Luke records it like this, "....But I have prayed for thee, that thy faith fail not..." The term "fail" used in the text comes from the Greek term *eclipto,* from which we borrow our word *eclipse*. During an eclipse, the Earth ends up separated from the sun. Jesus is saying to Peter, "No matter how severe the attack launched at you by satan, do not let anything separate you from me; after all, I am the Son!" In other words, stay with the Lord no matter what; you will discover He will never leave you alone.

Today's Push
Remember this: You can't walk away from the Lord because God is omnipresent and everywhere. In times of satanic attack, the enemy can convince you to say no to God and turn your back on Him. Receive these words of wisdom as you study this lesson today: stay with the Lord! He will not fail you. READ - Deut. 31:8

Today's Prayer
There have been times, O God, when I have felt all alone. In those moments, I had mixed emotions, scattered thoughts, and doubts about some things I was once sure of. But I want you to know right now that I plan to hold your hand until the day I meet you face to face. I love you, Lord.

In The Name of Jesus, Amen.

WEEK 13: Help Me Handle Satanic Attacks Launched Against Me

Day 6

NOW THAT YOU HAVE MADE IT HELP SOMEBODY ELSE GET THROUGH!

Today's Passage

And the Lord said, Simon, Simon, behold, Satan hath desired to have you, that he may sift you as wheat: But I have prayed for thee, that thy faith fail not: and when thou art converted, strengthen thy brethren (St. Luke 22:31-32).

Today's Point To Practice

While preaching a revival one evening in the Windy City of Chicago, a very tall, muscular man started to rejoice in the Lord while the choir sang a song about God's grace. His hands were lifted in praise, and his gratitude was on public display for heaven to see and others to observe. However, the man sitting beside him did not move one muscle.

After worship, I had the pleasure of shaking the hands of both men. It was then that I asked the gentleman who was rejoicing why he was so happy. His answer floored me. He told me he had just been diagnosed with prostate cancer. I thought I misunderstood him, so I inquired again, and he repeated his diagnosis a second time. Okay, so now I'm confused. You see, you don't usually see believers shouting praises to the Lord for a recent prostate cancer diagnosis. He noticed the confused and perplexed look on my face, so he added a brief explanation. He said, "Pastor, I'm shouting in here, man, and giving God the glory because I was diagnosed, but my friend that I was sitting next to has just been healed from the same thing. If the good Lord could heal him, He can do it for me!"

You see, one brother who had been healed from prostate cancer told his friend that God healed him and brought him to church immediately following his diagnosis.

This is the feeling expressed in the text. Jesus tells Peter this same thing in a different way. Jesus says, "... And when thou art converted, strengthen thy brethren." The Lord tells Peter, "When you make it through the attack that has been launched against you (and you will make it because I am with you), what I want you to do is turn around and help those who are going through an attack endure it the same way you have."

Today's Push

The Lord did not help you get through your attack only for you. He did it with other people in mind. Your attack is not an isolated incident. There are others who are struggling and dealing

WEEK 13: Help Me Handle Satanic Attacks Launched Against Me

with issues, and the Lord wants to use your life and your testimony to tell them just how able He is. READ - Rev. 12:11

Today's Prayer

Heavenly Father, use my life for your glory. You have done so much for me and brought me through so much. I have been through so many attacks by the enemy. Thank you for blessing me the way you have, and I will let my light shine so that those in the darkness of an attack can see you through me.

In The Name of Jesus, Amen.

WEEK 13: Help Me Handle Satanic Attacks Launched Against Me

Day 7

NEVER FORGET THIS: HE'S PREPARING YOU!

Today's Passage
And the Lord said, Simon, Simon, behold, Satan hath desired to have you, that he may sift you as wheat: But I have prayed for thee, that thy faith fail not: and when thou art converted, strengthen thy brethren (St. Luke 22:31-32).

Today's Point To Practice
In our study passage this week, Jesus warns Peter about an upcoming satanic attack. The attack is being allowed by the Lord, who could have stopped the entire thing. However, the Lord does not prevent it because He prepares Peter for something greater. In fact, the strength needed for his next assignment was gained through the trial he will soon face.

What is his next assignment, you ask? God is preparing Peter for Pentecost! That is the grand opening for the Lord's church on Earth! Peter will be the keynote speaker. You can read his keynote address in Acts 2. It was so masterful that 3,000 people came to Christ when he finished speaking.

Of course, Peter did not know it while the enemy attacked him, but he was learning lessons he would need for the work yet to come. He learned the lesson of trusting the Lord's will, and everything else was falling apart. He learned the lesson of watching the Lord work it out when he could no longer work on it. He learned the lesson of staying with Jesus Christ no matter what. These were invaluable lessons Peter had to have to push the kingdom of God forward on Earth!

Today's Push
Are you dealing with an attack on your life right now? Is the enemy doing his best to have your life fall to pieces? Are you in a place of spiritual darkness? Do not panic! Hold on to the Lord's unchanging hand, and know that you will come out of it stronger than ever! And the great news is that He is preparing you for your next assignment, which will bring out the best in you for His glory! READ - Romans 12:1-2

Today's Prayer
Eternal God, I ask you to continue to prepare me. Cause my tears to become my joy, make my struggles my strength, and take my enemies and make them my footstool.

In The Name of Jesus, Amen.

WEEK 14: Help Me Handle How I Treat Him

Day 1

GOD WANTS YOUR VERY BEST!

Our Passage of Study
And being in Bethany in the house of Simon, the leper, as he sat at meat, there came a woman having an alabaster box of ointment of Spikenard very precious, and she broke the box and poured it on his head. And there were some that had indignation within themselves, and said, Why was this waste of the ointment made? For it might have been sold for more than three hundred pence and have been given to the poor. And they murmured against her. And Jesus said, Let her alone; why trouble ye her? she hath wrought a good work on me. For ye have the poor with you always, and whensoever ye will ye may do them good: but me ye have not always. She hath done what she could: she is come aforehand to anoint my body to the burying. Verily I say unto you, Wheresoever this gospel shall be preached throughout the whole world, this also that she hath done shall be spoken of for a memorial of her (St. Mark 14:3-9).

Today's Parable
In the summer of 2024, I journeyed to Ghana, West Africa, to the remote village of Konkori with a group of Christians from our church and region to celebrate the development of a community center, a school for children, and fresh running water from a tower that was all built through resources from our church family and gracious community donors. The trip was remarkable, the flight was excellent, and the people of the village were kind, hospitable, and welcoming.

Upon arrival to the village, we were met by wonderful people who took us to meet the King of the village of Konkori, whose name is Nano Nyboi. The King was a good-looking octogenarian with a chiseled chin and strong shoulders, even at his age. As we walked to the King's palace, drummers played, the people sang songs in their language, and our missionaries walked in utter amazement at what the Lord was doing with us in the motherland. As we approached the village, we were told to enter the outer porch of the King's palace and have a seat.

A few moments after taking a seat, shaking a few hands, and sharing gracious greetings, we were graced with the presence of their King. There he stood, and for the first time in my life, I was in the presence of a king on Earth. You see, as an American, I am unfamiliar with kings. We have Presidents, Senators, Congressmen, Governors, Aldermen, Counselors, Mayors, and others. But a king we do not have. I did not know what to do. I did not know whether to bow, sit, stand, clap, shout, or hold my peace. Even though I did not know quite what to do, here's what I am sure of: you had to be careful how you were to handle him.

WEEK 14: Help Me Handle How I Treat Him

You do not handle a king like an ordinary citizen because the King is not ordinary. The power of the government rests, rules, and remains in the heart of the King! With this in mind, you give a king your very best. Not just any gift will do. In fact, either give the King your best or do not give him anything at all.

For the next few days, we will be looking at the passage listed for this week's study. It details and describes how Mary, the sister of Lazarus, entreats Jesus by pouring a precious ointment called Spikenard all over Him. This aromatic perfume was worth a centurion soldier's annual salary—it was expensive, to say the least. And this is what she pours on the head of our Lord because, in her heart, she believes He is worthy to be praised.

Today's Prayer
Lord of glory, God of heaven, I desire to give you not just my best but also my life. When I consider how you died to save me, it is my decision and intention to serve you with everything that I have to offer. Lord Jesus, you are my King, and I love you with everything in me.

In The Name of Jesus, Amen.

WEEK 14: Help Me Handle How I Treat Him

Day 2

YOU OWE HIM AND YOU KNOW IT!

Today's Passage

And being in Bethany in the house of Simon the leper, as he sat at meat, there came a woman having an alabaster box of ointment of Spikenard very precious; and she brake the box, and poured it on his head. And there were some that had indignation within themselves, and said, Why was this waste of the ointment made? For it might have been sold for more than three hundred pence and have been given to the poor. And they murmured against her. And Jesus said, Let her alone; why trouble ye her? she hath wrought a good work on me. For ye have the poor with you always, and whensoever ye will ye may do them good: but me ye have not always. She hath done what she could: she is come aforehand to anoint my body to the burying. Verily I say unto you, Wheresoever this gospel shall be preached throughout the whole world, this also that she hath done shall be spoken of for a memorial of her (St. Mark 14:3-9, KJV).

Today's Point To Practice

Mary is an uninvited guest when she enters this banquet at Simon the Lepers' house. The disciples are there to receive dinner from the Lord, but she shows up with a different agenda. She is there to give Him her very precious spikenard oil. It was precious because it was so pricey. The shocking truth from the passage is that she did not break the bottle and give the Lord a portion. She broke the bottle and gave Jesus everything.

There is a reason why she behaves like this. When Mary had the most challenging time, Jesus stepped in and fixed what no one else could repair. Mary had a brother whose name was Lazarus (St. John 11). He got very sick and died. Of course, Mary and Martha, her sister, called for Jesus to come and help him, but Jesus did not come when they wanted Him to. By the time Jesus arrives, it appears that all hope is gone, and nothing can be done. The Lord gets to the tomb of Lazarus and calls him by his name, and he is resurrected and brought back to life.

Mary never forgot what the Lord did for her and her family. During her time of brokenness, the Lord helped her, so she did not mind breaking her vessel just to bless Him. In other words, she owed Him, and she knew it!

Today's Push

Here's a wonderful question to ponder as you study God's Word today: Have you ever stopped to consider how much you owe God? If you are like those with good sense, you know that you

WEEK 14: Help Me Handle How I Treat Him

owe Him everything because He gave you everything when Jesus was sacrificed on the cross. In fact, here's the truth: We owe Him big time!

READ - Romans 8:12-17

Today's Prayer

Merciful Master, I owe you more than I can ever repay. When I pause to consider the sins you have forgiven, the grace you have bestowed, the love you have shared, and the doors you have opened, my soul cries out, "Thank you!"

In The Name of Jesus, Amen.

WEEK 14: Help Me Handle How I Treat Him

Day 3

PREPARE TO BE CRITICIZED!

Today's Passage

And being in Bethany in the house of Simon the leper, as he sat at meat, there came a woman having an alabaster box of ointment of Spikenard very precious; and she brake the box, and poured it on his head. And there were some that had indignation within themselves, and said, Why was this waste of the ointment made? For it might have been sold for more than three hundred pence and have been given to the poor. And they murmured against her. And Jesus said, Let her alone; why trouble ye her? she hath wrought a good work on me. For ye have the poor with you always, and whensoever ye will ye may do them good: but me ye have not always. She hath done what she could: she is come aforehand to anoint my body to the burying. Verily I say unto you, Wheresoever this gospel shall be preached throughout the whole world, this also that she hath done shall be spoken of for a memorial of her (St. Mark 14:3-9).

Today's Point To Practice

A good friend of mine, Darlene, works for a chemical plant on the eastern seaboard. She is often surrounded by somewhat chauvinistic men and hit by people who have something to say about the Bible that she keeps on her desk. By now, you have to know that D (what we called Darlene while we were in school) is a devout Christian. She is one of the forthright sisters who is totally unashamed and unapologetic about her love for Jesus Christ.

One day, while preparing to eat her lunch in the break room, she bowed for a whisper of thanksgiving for the food she was about to receive. When she lifted her head to receive what she had thanked the Lord for, she was eyed by several people looking at her as if she were a mad woman. Suddenly, new rules emerged regarding "religious insignia in the workplace." Several supervisors held meetings to discuss newfound "company policies" on what was permissible at work regarding religious activity and what was not. In short, it was an attack against Darlene by those who had a problem with her faith in God.

In our lesson today, the Disciples openly criticize Mary because of her love and faith for Jesus Christ. So much so that they called what she gave Him a waste. The word for *waste* in Greek comes from the term *Apollyon*. It was a reference to hell and Hades. They were saying this carrying-on had to be from hell in some way. They missed that her gift to the Lord did not come from hell, but she had been through hell to get where she was in Christ. Her journey had been anything but easy.

WEEK 14: Help Me Handle How I Treat Him

In this last and evil day, it will become increasingly unpopular to love the Lord. You can expect to be criticized if you love Him with your whole heart, outwardly and inwardly.

Today's Push
When walking according to the Lord's Word, you will know because others will criticize you.

READ - 2 Timothy 3:12

Today's Prayer
Lord thank you for those who speak evil of me because of my love for you. If you could take nails for me, the least I can do for you is stand firm in the criticisms of those who do not treasure your sacrifice for us at the cross. I will stand for you until the day I die. I owe you that much.

In The Name of Jesus, Amen.

WEEK 14: Help Me Handle How I Treat Him

Day 4

TREAT HIM LIKE A KING!

Today's Passage

And being in Bethany in the house of Simon the leper, as he sat at meat, there came a woman having an alabaster box of ointment of Spikenard very precious; and she brake the box, and poured it on his head. And there were some that had indignation within themselves, and said, Why was this waste of the ointment made? For it might have been sold for more than three hundred pence and have been given to the poor. And they murmured against her. And Jesus said, Let her alone; why trouble ye her? she hath wrought a good work on me. For ye have the poor with you always, and whensoever ye will ye may do them good: but me ye have not always. She hath done what she could: she is come aforehand to anoint my body to the burying. Verily I say unto you, Wheresoever this gospel shall be preached throughout the whole world, this also that she hath done shall be spoken of for a memorial of her (St. Mark 14:3-9).

Today's Point To Practice

It was the Holiday Season of 2008, and it was a somewhat strained season for the Adolph family. My mother had transitioned from time and slipped into eternity. My Father was not in the best of health, and problems were rising on every hand. Have you ever had a season where it felt like you were going from one hurt to another? It was that kind of season for us. The absence of Momma weighed heavily on our hearts. We were all trying to do our best to keep the family moving, but it was easier said than done.

We celebrate Christmas on Christmas Eve. We gather at my sister's house for food, fellowship, and the exchange of gifts when my younger brother Ron suddenly says, "Yall, we have a lot to be thankful for because Daddy is still living, and we know Momma is in a much better place, so what we are going to do is spoil him rotten. We are going to treat him like a king!"

From that moment on, we showered each other with love, laughter, faith, and family, but more than anything else, we treated Daddy like a King! If he wanted cake, he got it (even though his glucose was too high); if he wanted pecan pie with vanilla ice cream, he got it. And, if he wanted a turkey wing with a bit of extra fat on it, we got it for him. Why? You treat a king like a King!

When Mary enters Simon's house, she shows up to treat Jesus not like a carpenter from Nazareth but like her King from eternal glory. She shows up with a gift that was used for the coronation of a king called Spikenard. It was an imported aromatic perfume from India. It was taken from

WEEK 14: Help Me Handle How I Treat Him

a small seaport plant that, when crushed, produced an extremely costly fragrant oil. Mary brings oil for her King because, in her heart, that's how she wants to treat him.

Today's Push
Never forget this: how you see Him is ultimately how you will treat Him! If you see Him as a nobody, you'll treat Him like a nobody. If you see Him as a weak, sorry leader, you'll treat Him like a weak, sorry leader. However, if you see Him as a King, you will ultimately treat Him as the King that He is!

READ - St. John 19:19-22

Today's Prayer
King Jesus, I bow before you because in my heart you are King of all Kings; you are Lord of all lords; you are Alpha and Omega, the Beginning and the End; the first and the last; the Amen and the proper conclusion to every matter. Thank you for allowing me to be your servant and to dwell in your presence.

In The Name of Jesus, Amen.

WEEK 14: Help Me Handle How I Treat Him

Day 5

YOU'RE DOING IT RIGHT WHEN……!

Today's Passage

And being in Bethany in the house of Simon the leper, as he sat at meat, there came a woman having an alabaster box of ointment of Spikenard very precious; and she brake the box, and poured it on his head. And there were some that had indignation within themselves, and said, Why was this waste of the ointment made? For it might have been sold for more than three hundred pence and have been given to the poor. And they murmured against her. And Jesus said, Let her alone; why trouble ye her? she hath wrought a good work on me. For ye have the poor with you always, and whensoever ye will ye may do them good: but me ye have not always. She hath done what she could: she is come aforehand to anoint my body to the burying. Verily I say unto you, Wheresoever this gospel shall be preached throughout the whole world, this also that she hath done shall be spoken of for a memorial of her (St. Mark 14:3-9).

Today's Point To Practice

I love being in the company of believers actively and passionately worshiping our God. Even though I should be a participant myself, I often find myself being a spectator. Don't judge me! But, I love watching Saints love the Lord who saved them in worship. With this in mind, I've seen just about everything. I've seen people blow whistles in church. That's right! I said whistles. I've seen people crash the lids of trash cans in church. I have even seen a lady with the Campbell's chicken soup can and a stick in church. She nearly beat that can to death. And on every occasion, here is what I have noticed. There are always people who think those who sincerely worship God are overdoing it. You will hear things like, "It doesn't take all of that."

I have concluded that if your worship honors the Lord and angers the adversary, you're doing it right. Don't pay any attention to what others say about it if your worship bothers some believers who refuse to give God praise and glory. Bless the Lord for the God that he is. You're doing it right. Don't let anyone stop you!

In our scripture study this week we find a woman whose name is Mary. She is the sister of Lazarus of Bethany. When she arrives at Simon Leper's house, she comes in to worship the Lord, who is her King. When she began to pour her oil upon his head, the beautiful fragrance of her perfume made the entire house smell wonderful. Yet, the disciples were bothered by her blessing the Lord. They even went as far as to say that what she offered him was a waste. They said the oil could have been sold, and the money could have been used to help the poor. Isn't it interesting? People will want to tell you what to do with the honor you desire to give God. Never let them do it.

WEEK 14: Help Me Handle How I Treat Him

I'm grateful that Mary decided to bless the Lord, who had blessed her uniquely. Believe it or not, she was doing it right!

Today's Push
Here's a good devotional question for you to grapple with as we look to study our passage for the week. How do you honor God in worship in a public setting? Do you lift your hands? Do you shout praises of acclamation? Do you sing songs that are pleasing to His heart? Whatever you do, do it so that when God sees you, He will send heaven a report that says you are doing it correctly!

READ - Psalms 34:1-5

Today's Prayer
I praise you, O God, forever and always! I bless your name and honor you for who you are and for what you have done. Thank you, Lord Jesus, for being the kind of King who would lay down His life for people like me to have a life to live. I will praise you, O God, forever and always!

In The Name of Jesus, Amen.

WEEK 14: Help Me Handle How I Treat Him

Day 6

DO IT BECAUSE YOU CAN!

Today's Passage

And being in Bethany in the house of Simon the leper, as he sat at meat, there came a woman having an alabaster box of ointment of Spikenard very precious; and she brake the box, and poured it on his head. And there were some that had indignation within themselves, and said, Why was this waste of the ointment made? For it might have been sold for more than three hundred pence and have been given to the poor. And they murmured against her. And Jesus said, Let her alone; why trouble ye her? she hath wrought a good work on me. For ye have the poor with you always, and whensoever ye will ye may do them good: but me ye have not always. She hath done what she could: she is come aforehand to anoint my body to the burying. Verily I say unto you, Wheresoever this gospel shall be preached throughout the whole world, this also that she hath done shall be spoken of for a memorial of her (St. Mark 14:3-9).

Today's Point To Practice

Most Christians misunderstand the act of worship that honors the Lord. We often approach the subject matter as if it is something we must do. Please understand this: worship is a primary function of the faithful. If you believe in Jesus Christ, you should spend your life worshiping him with your service, in total submission, and for his sacrifice.

We get things twisted because we feel that we must worship. However, looking closely at what Mary offers Jesus in this week's study session should shift our minds slightly. Mary does not worship Jesus in this story because she has to. She could've been doing other things. If you look closely at her honoring the Lord, you will discover that she does it not because she has to but simply because she can. Her legs functioned adequately, so she walked to the dwelling place where He was. Her arms still moved, so she poured the oil on His head with them. And because she was blessed with oil, she blessed Him.

The picture here is very significant. Sometimes, you should honor God for who He is just because you can!

Today's Push

Sing because you can! Clap because you can! Pray because you can! Dance because you can! Serve because you can! Worship because you can!

READ-PALMS Psalms 100

WEEK 14: Help Me Handle How I Treat Him

Today's Prayer

God, I realize that you do not have to allow my worship in your presence. I could be incapacitated and unable to offer you anything, as some are. But you have graced me with enough health and soundness of mind to offer you the best that I can give you in service. Please know that I plan to do it just because I can.

In The Name of Jesus, Amen.

WEEK 14: Help Me Handle How I Treat Him

Day 7

WHAT HE DESERVES IS A WORSHIP THAT'S REAL!

Today's Passage

And being in Bethany in the house of Simon the leper, as he sat at meat, there came a woman having an alabaster box of ointment of Spikenard very precious; and she brake the box, and poured it on his head. And there were some that had indignation within themselves, and said, Why was this waste of the ointment made? For it might have been sold for more than three hundred pence and have been given to the poor. And they murmured against her. And Jesus said, Let her alone; why trouble ye her? she hath wrought a good work on me. For ye have the poor with you always, and whensoever ye will ye may do them good: but me ye have not always. She hath done what she could: she is come aforehand to anoint my body to the burying. Verily I say unto you, Wheresoever this gospel shall be preached throughout the whole world, this also that she hath done shall be spoken of for a memorial of her (St. Mark 14:3-9).

Today's Point To Practice

As this study week concludes, I want to share something about this story you should never forget. Jesus says, "Verily I say unto you, Wheresoever this gospel shall be preached throughout the whole world, this also that she hath done shall be spoken of for a memorial of her." What does He mean by this statement? Here's the news that is a blessing for those who believe. Mary's worship was like none other because it was the worship Jesus took with Him to the cross.

Often, we hear Bible readers say that Jesus went to the cross alone. But this is not true at all. When the Lord leaves the meal at Simon's house, He is headed to Calvary for our sins. And everywhere He went, the fragrant smell of Spikenard went with Him. When He stood before Pilate, they had to smell Spikenard. When He was marched from judgment hall to judgment hall, they had to smell Spikenard. And when He was crucified, they had to smell Spikenard.

Do you remember the Roman soldiers who gambled for Jesus' clothing (St. Matthew 27:35)? Do you know why they did it? They were covered in Spikenard, and that fragrance gave Jesus' clothes value.

Mary's extraordinary worship was so outstanding in the eyes of the Lord that Jesus declared that her honoring Him would walk alongside the Gospel message itself as a memorial of her. In short, it was sincere, devout, and real worship.

WEEK 14: Help Me Handle How I Treat Him

Today's Push
God deserves our best because He gave His best to us in the person of His Son, Jesus. With this in mind, give the Lord what is real, pure, and authentic. Your love for Him will always give Him the glory that He truly deserves.

READ - Psalms 72:19

Today's Prayer
May the glory that I offer you with the life you have given me to live be yours forever and ever, O God.

In The Name of Jesus, Amen.

WEEK 15: Help Me Handle My Hurt

Day 1

God's Word For You Today: HATING YOU CAN KILL ME!

Our Passage of Study
Then said Jesus, Father, forgive them, for they know not what they do. And they parted his raiment, and cast lots (St. Luke 23:34).

Today's Parable
It was the most vicious murder that has ever taken place in Beaumont, Texas. The victim was not just shot, stabbed, or beaten to death; she was recklessly and demonically taken from her family by what was her so-called boyfriend. The details of this murder are too gruesome to recount in this book. However, what is worth lifting for us to consider is the hurt that it caused her family. Her family was crushed beyond measure, to say the least. And, from their hurt grew anger; from anger hostility; hostility became bitterness; from bitterness a hatred that was nearly justified.

Ronnie Leday, the victim's older brother, serves as a Deacon at the Antioch Church, where I am privileged to be Pastor. When the family was due in court to finally come face-to-face with the man who committed this heinous crime, as he took a seat in the courtroom that day, he appeared arrogant, pompous, and totally unremorseful. He showed no sign of pity, empathy, apathy, or compassion whatsoever. The Judge then asked this murderer if he had anything to say, and he looked at the Judge as if to say, "Can you just hurry up and sentence me because I have things to do, and you are slowing me down."

The family was bothered by this, and hurt, and anger filled the courtroom thick enough for you to cut with a knife and feel it. The Judge then looked up and asked the family if anyone wanted to speak to the man who had been charged with the murder of their loved one. Deacon Leday rose to his feet and approached the lectern in the heart of the courtroom. I have never seen or heard anything like this before in my life. It was as if I was watching a movie on a Hollywood screen. When Deacon Leday gets to the mic, He says to the man sitting before him, "I do not hate you for what you have done to my sister. My God controls this entire situation and everything you have done. For me to hate you puts my life in bondage, and I'm free, and I refuse to be bound. I'm praying for your soul, and I'm asking God to save you and heal you."

It was a move of God in that courtroom—like the air being let out of a tire. The hatred that was there was met by a much greater power, and it was the power of forgiveness.

WEEK 15: Help Me Handle My Hurt

In our lesson this week, we will learn from our Lord on the cross as He asks for forgiveness for the people who put Him to death. His words are piercing and poignant, yet they are real and redemptive. "Then said Jesus, Father, forgive them; for they know not what they do." (St. Luke 23:34a).

Today's Prayer

Lord, I have been wounded by people who have intentionally done things to hurt me, and I know it. There have been times and moments when my dislike for them slipped into hatred. Heal me and make me whole, O God. Thank you for healing me and blessing me with the power to forgive.

In The Name of Jesus, Amen.

WEEK 15: Help Me Handle My Hurt

Day 2

FORGIVENESS IS NOT FORGETTING WHAT HAPPENED!

Today's Passage
Then said Jesus, Father, forgive them, for they know not what they do. And they parted his raiment, and cast lots (St. Luke 23:34).

Today's Point To Practice
The phrase "forgive and forget" is nowhere in the Bible. We have heard it all of our lives, and it sounds good, but it is not practical. Think about it for a moment. Why would God give you a memory if He wanted you to forgive and forget? The idea of trying to make this happen is just different from the Lord's way. His way is greater, deeper, and more meaningful than ever imagined. God wants you to get to a place of real forgiveness, which means remembering what happened without the pain. That's true forgiveness. It happens when you say, "I can remember everything they did, but it no longer bothers or hurts me anymore."

When true forgiveness occurs, God grows you to a place where you start to feel pity and compassion for the people who did you harm. You reach a place where you feel sorry for them.

Today's Push
To forgive doesn't mean you have to forget. It means you need to remember without the pain. If it still hurts when you consider the damage done, stay near the Lord because He is not through healing you yet. When your healing is finished, you will recount what was done and what was said, but it will not hurt you any longer.

READ - Isaiah 43:25

Today's Prayer
Lord Jesus, please grow me to the point in your strength that I can forgive like I should. Sometimes, it is a struggle for me, and I admit it. I thank you for being patient with me and not giving up on me.

In The Name of Jesus, Amen.

WEEK 15: Help Me Handle My Hurt Day 3

IF YOU NEED IT YOU HAVE TO GIVE IT!

Today's Passage

Then said Jesus, Father, forgive them, for they know not what they do. And they parted his raiment, and cast lots (St. Luke 23:34).

Today's Point To Practice

Take a moment and think about some things you need forgiveness for. Are you thinking about it yet? Consider some people you hurt, lied to, or damaged. Think about the punishment that you deserve. Here's the best news of the day: Imagine God looking at you and saying, "I will forgive all of your sins, wrongdoings, mishaps, mess-ups, bad habits, and secret evil, but you must first forgive those who wronged you."

Forgiveness is a Kingdom law based on the principle of reciprocity. You must first let others have it so you can receive it from God when needed.

Here's a good devotional question to ask right about now. How badly do you need the Lord to forgive your sins and clean your slate? If you need forgiveness, you must let others who have hurt you go.

Today's Push

Real forgiveness brings you to where you let others go because you need the Lord to let you make it. Here's the secret to gaining forgiveness from the Lord: never forget it, and let them go!

READ - St. Matthew 6:14-15

Today's Prayer

O God, I know I need forgiveness from you. I have had my share of mistakes and errors. I can hide from others, but I cannot hide from you. Lord, you know me up close and from a distance. You know me for who I am. Help me let others go so I can find the grace you need to forgive me.

In The Name of Jesus, Amen.

WEEK 15: Help Me Handle My Hurt

Day 4

FORGIVENESS IS NOT FOR THEM IT'S FOR YOU!

Today's Passage
Then said Jesus, Father, forgive them, for they know not what they do. And they parted his raiment, and cast lots (St. Luke 23:34).

Today's Point To Practice
Jesus is now on the cross. He's beaten, punched, spat upon, lied on, and judged falsely. His body had been nailed to a tree while He was still alive. The Roman Soldiers shake the cross to ensure His flesh will hold His weight and not give way. They tilt the cross forward so that He has to push down on His feet and pull up on His hands to get another breath of air into His lungs just to stay alive. He looks down at the very men who are responsible for nailing Him, piercing Him, and scouring Him. He does not look towards heaven and say, "Father, get these scoundrels, especially this guy to my left with the hammer in his hand." Jesus does not say this at all. He does say, "Father forgive them…"

With this in mind, our Lord understands the personal nature of forgiveness. He knows that forgiveness is not only for the men who harmed Him but also for Him. Jesus knows that this is personal, so He treats it that way. Unforgiveness can make you bitter, mean, angry, vengeful, and joyless, sometimes feeling hopeless. That is why forgiveness is so powerful. It is a personal act that leads to healing and restoration.

Today's Push
Here is the lesson for you to hold on to through today and the rest of your life: Forgiving others blesses you! If you want to bless yourself, decrease your stress level, and increase your joy, forgive those who have sought to harm you and succeeded.

READ - St. Matthew 6:9-15

Today's Prayer
Unto thee, O God, do I place my hope. My desire right now, Lord, is to bless myself by forgiving people who have done me wrong. Give me the strength to do it, and if I'm too weak, give me more of you so I'll have less of me when I need you the most.

In The Name of Jesus, Amen.

WEEK 15: Help Me Handle My Hurt

Day 5

THE SECRET TO DOING THIS IS......YOU CAN'T, BUT GOD CAN!

Today's Passage
Then said Jesus, Father, forgive them, for they know not what they do. And they parted his raiment, and cast lots (St. Luke 23:34).

Today's Point To Practice
The miracle of forgiveness is to remember this one huge secret. It determines whether you succeed or fail, overcome or become overwhelmed. Here it is, and never forget it; you do not possess the ability alone to forgive. The Holy Spirit within you empowers you with the ability to do it. Without the Lord dwelling in your life, you will never forgive anyone. Evidence of God's presence working within you is God doing things through you that you know you otherwise would not or could not do without Him.

One of the members of our church saw her ex-husband walking down a dark street one night with a gas can in his hand. His truck had run empty. He abused her both verbally and physically. She hated him for a season, and thoughts of him angered her. When she saw him initially, all types of deviant thoughts crossed her mind, but the Lord within her led her to pick him up and take him to the gas station, pay for his gas, and then drop him off at his truck.

She told me, "Pastor Adolph, it had to be God! Nothing in me could have done that. I felt calm covering me and needed to help him, and God did it! It was the Lord, Pastor, it was the Lord!"

Today's Push
You will never forgive anyone without God's power operating fully in your life. When He is ever present, you will sense His power, and supernatural things will happen, like the power to forgive.

READ - St. Matthew 19:26

Today's Prayer
Lord, I pray for you to empower me like never before so that the power to forgive lives in me just as it did in you when you were on the cross.

In The Name of Jesus, Amen.

WEEK 15: Help Me Handle My Hurt

Day 6

HOLDING A GRUDGE IS HOLDING YOU HOSTAGE!

Today's Passage
Then said Jesus, Father, forgive them, for they know not what they do. And they parted his raiment, and cast lots (St. Luke 23:34).

Today's Point To Practice
Imagine for a moment that there is a hostage situation taking place right now. There is a person wearing handcuffs who is not permitted to go free. They are shackled and bound and living a total nightmare. Everywhere they go, the shackles that they wear go with them. It is painful, to say the least. It is a struggle, and no one knows it. Can you see them? Use your imagination.

Now imagine that the person wearing the shackles is you. The bitterness of unforgiveness puts shackles on you that no one can see, but they are there. They are hidden beneath the eyeliner and the weave. They are beneath the surface of the chiseled chin and the nice clothing. Unforgiveness is dangerous because it imprisons you without you being aware that you are even incarcerated.

The great news of the day, however, is that you can decide to let the prisoner go free! True forgiveness happens when you realize that holding a grudge is holding you hostage, and you decide to lose the shackles and open the prison door to let the inmate go free, only to discover that you were the prisoner wearing the shackles.

Today's Push
Are you the kind of person who holds a grudge? Are you holding a grudge right now? If you answered yes, you are in shackles and don't even know it. But you do not have to remain in this state. You can decide to forgive, and when you do it, the shackles of unforgiveness will disappear, and so will your grudge.

READ - James 5:9-12

Today's Prayer
I'm so tired of living in bondage, Lord. Be my liberator and emancipator O God. Please, I pray, let the shackles of any grudge that could be attaching itself to my life fall by the wayside of my life and never be connected to me again.

In The Name of Jesus, Amen.

WEEK 15: Help Me Handle My Hurt

Day 7

God's Word For You Today: LET IT GO!

Today's Passage
Then said Jesus, Father, forgive them, for they know not what they do. And they parted his raiment, and cast lots (St. Luke 23:34).

Today's Point To Practice
The Lord favored me to do a revival in Dubai, which was an incredible experience. After the revival services, I spent a few days touring and enjoying the region. One day, my tour guide took me to a hot-air balloon site where tourists could ride over parts of the desert in a hot-air balloon. I chose to remain on the ground where the Lord had planted me. Nevertheless, I could not help but notice several balloons taking off and soaring at incredible heights. As I considered the height of each balloon, I noticed that the people responsible for flying these old-school aeronautical baskets mid-air kept dumping these sandbags over the side. The more sandbags they dropped, the higher the hot air balloon flew.

Unforgiveness is heavy, like sandbags attached to a hot air balloon. Jesus had to have understood this one emphatic principle. He knew He would die and need to be resurrected from the dead, so what He did was wise. He dropped the sandbags of hatred, malice, contempt, bitterness, resentment, vengeance, and unforgiveness so that nothing would hold Him down when resurrection morning came. For the final time of this week's study, hear Jesus' words regarding forgiveness: "Father, forgive them; for they know not what they do." In short, what Jesus did from the cross is exactly what the hot air balloon conductors did that caused them to rise from the Earth. They let the heavy stuff go!

Today's Push
What sense does it make to hold onto the heavy burden of unforgiveness when you can choose to let it go? Here's some solid advice and spiritual wisdom that will last you a lifetime: let it go!

READ - Genesis 50:15-20

Today's Prayer
Lord Jesus, just as you rose from the grave without the heaviness resting upon you, I pray that you allow me to rise each day without the heavy burden of unforgiveness.

In The Name of Jesus, Amen.

WEEK 16: Help Me Handle It When What I Need Is an Upset

Day 1

SOMETIMES THINGS GO FROM BAD TO WORST!

Our Passage of Study
In the end of the sabbath, as it began to dawn toward the first day of the week, came Mary Magdalene and the other Mary to see the sepulchre. And, behold, there was a great earthquake: for the angel of the Lord descended from heaven, and came and rolled back the stone from the door, and sat upon it. His countenance was like lightning, and his raiment white as snow: And for fear of him the keepers did shake, and became as dead men. And the angel answered and said unto the women, Fear not ye: for I know that ye seek Jesus, which was crucified. He is not here, for he is risen, as he said. Come, see the place where the Lord lay. And go quickly, and tell his disciples that he is risen from the dead; and, behold, he goeth before you into Galilee; there shall ye see him: lo, I have told you. And they departed quickly from the sepulchre with fear and great joy; and did run to bring his disciples word. And as they went to tell his disciples, behold, Jesus met them, saying, All hail. And they came and held him by the feet, and worshipped him (St. Matthew 28:1-9).

Today's Parable
Sometimes, God permits and allows bad things to happen to good people. There were even times when things in life go from bad to worse. During seasons like this, we have more questions for God than ever. In fact, we have more question marks than we do exclamation points. Have you ever been here before? Has life ever put you in a place where things went from bad to worse? Have you ever prayed and asked God for help, and it seemed He was not listening?

Such was the case in the life of Sylvia Ann Brown. She was diagnosed with a very strange neurological disorder that caused multiple problems in her body. She often complained of tingling, soreness, and tightness in her lower extremities. When doctors finally got her diagnosed, it was with a disease that she could not pronounce, from a doctor that she did not know, with a pathology she did not understand. That's bad enough, right? However, things got worse. You see, due to her illness, she could not work. Her employer of 22 years gave her a release form with no benefits attached. That's bad enough, isn't it? Wait, it gets worse. When she lost her job, she also lost her townhome, which forced her to move into her mother's house for safety, lodging, and medical reasons. That's bad enough, right? Well, things still get worse. They repossessed her car, even though she had been making partial payments on her monthly note.

WEEK 16: Help Me Handle It When What I Need Is an Upset

Failing health, financial struggle, lack of transportation, and no place to live can make life a nightmare. Yet to speak Sylvia Ann was always a blessing! Even when life seemingly took more from her than she had left, she never complained. On one occasion, I spoke with her, and before we prayed, she told me how blessed she was. She exclaimed with vigor how thankful she was to be alive and to walk and have her mind. It gave me a new perspective on Christian suffering. Here's the point for today's lesson: there are times when God allows life to go from bad to worse. And faithful Christians do not complain but find the strength to look towards heaven, beyond their human condition, and say thank you!

In our study passage for this week, we will look at Jesus on the cross. He never complains, though his suffering is immense. He never blames anyone, yet his suffering is beyond human comprehension. He never gives up until he takes his final breath and dies. The shout in this narrative is that even though things went from bad to worse, he was faithful, no matter what.

Here's a worthwhile question as we begin our final week together. How much can you endure before you start complaining about your current conditions? Can God trust you with human sorrow and allow things to go from bad to worse?

Today's Prayer
Lord, help me hold on when life makes me want to let go. Help me trust you when the heartache that I am dealing with makes no sense.

In The Name of Jesus, Amen.

WEEK 16: Help Me Handle It When What I Need Is an Upset

Day 2

JUST BECAUSE IT LOOKS BAD DOESN'T MEAN IT WILL END THAT WAY!

Today's Passage
In the end of the sabbath, as it began to dawn toward the first day of the week, came Mary Magdalene and the other Mary to see the sepulchre. And, behold, there was a great earthquake: for the angel of the Lord descended from heaven, and came and rolled back the stone from the door, and sat upon it. His countenance was like lightning, and his raiment white as snow: And for fear of him the keepers did shake, and became as dead men. And the angel answered and said unto the women, Fear not ye: for I know that ye seek Jesus, which was crucified. He is not here, for he is risen, as he said. Come, see the place where the Lord lay. And go quickly, and tell his disciples that he is risen from the dead; and, behold, he goeth before you into Galilee; there shall ye see him: lo, I have told you. And they departed quickly from the sepulchre with fear and great joy; and did run to bring his disciples word. And as they went to tell his disciples, behold, Jesus met them, saying, All hail. And they came and held him by the feet, and worshipped him (St. Matthew 28:1-9).

Today's Point To Practice
The day had been long, and the night even longer. Jesus has been put to death like a criminal on a cross, and things do not look too good for those who have followed Him. However, a remnant of faithful women press their way to the tomb early Sunday morning. In the Matthian passage above, two women are mentioned. One of the women is listed with specificity. She is Mary Magdalene. The second Mary is listed in generality. She is called "the other Mary." It stands to reason to ask who this "other Mary" is. I contend that it is Mary, the mother of Jesus. After all, like a good mother, she has been there with Him for every occasion, from His birth to His death. Why would she not show up at His grave?

The blessed news today for our time of study is that by the time these two women reach the gravesite of our Lord, what they find is nothing short of a miracle! They encounter an earth that has been shaken but not stirred. And they discover an angel with an announcement that Christians around the world still declare to this day: "He is not here!"

The moral of today's lesson is this: Just because it looks bad does not mean it will end that way.

WEEK 16: Help Me Handle It When What I Need Is an Upset

Today's Push

Here's something you should always remember as a believer in Jesus Christ: God works in the dark just as He does in the light. Hold on when it's dark, knowing that the tide will turn, life will shift, and things will get better!

READ - Romans 8:28

Today's Prayer

O God, I have had some dark days in my life, and I can testify to you in prayer that they did not remain dark. Your presence caused me to have some light even when I could not see my way through. Teach me how to endure, Lord. This is my sincere supplication and prayerful petition.

In The Name of Jesus, Amen.

WEEK 16: Help Me Handle It When What I Need Is an Upset

Day 3

LET YOUR ENEMIES DO THEIR PART!

Today's Passage
In the end of the sabbath, as it began to dawn toward the first day of the week, came Mary Magdalene and the other Mary to see the sepulchre. And, behold, there was a great earthquake: for the angel of the Lord descended from heaven, and came and rolled back the stone from the door, and sat upon it. His countenance was like lightning, and his raiment white as snow: And for fear of him the keepers did shake, and became as dead men. And the angel answered and said unto the women, Fear not ye: for I know that ye seek Jesus, which was crucified. He is not here, for he is risen, as he said. Come, see the place where the Lord lay. And go quickly, and tell his disciples that he is risen from the dead; and, behold, he goeth before you into Galilee; there shall ye see him: lo, I have told you. And they departed quickly from the sepulchre with fear and great joy; and did run to bring his disciples word. And as they went to tell his disciples, behold, Jesus met them, saying, All hail. And they came and held him by the feet, and worshipped him (St. Matthew 28:1-9).

Today's Point To Practice
Okay, let's just go ahead and address the large pink elephant sitting at the end of the table that no one wants to say anything about. As a believer in Jesus Christ, God allows you to have enemies. God permits haters. He allows people that despise you and want to see discomfort come your way. In fact, not only does God allow them into your life, but there are times when He orders them in your direction. He sends them!

When Jesus was being nailed to the cross, the men who nailed Him were on assignment. They were summoned by God the Father to do what they were doing, and there was no way around it. The man who swung the hammer. The guy with the nails. The man who made the cross. The men who punched Him in the face and spat upon Him. They were all doing what God allowed them to do. Why did God the Father allow this kind of thing to happen? Here's the easy answer: It should cause you to see people who have hurt you differently. If these men do not do their job, Jesus does not die, and there is no resurrection!

Thank God they did their job well! The report from the hill is that He died!! They did not take His life; He laid it down, and because Jesus is God the Son, He had the power to pick it back up again!

WEEK 16: Help Me Handle It When What I Need Is an Upset

Today's Push

When your enemies really hurt you, remember this: they are doing their job! You stay focused and do your job. Endure, persevere, and overcome!

READ - 2 Cor. 4:8-9, KJV

Today's Prayer

Lord Jesus, knowing that you had enemies makes me know that I will never be exempt from them. Yet I ask you for the strength to endure the evil they bring my way. Cause me to find favor in your sight and strength from your throne is my humble prayer.

In The Name of Jesus, Amen.

WEEK 16: Help Me Handle It When What I Need Is an Upset

Day 4

DECLARE YOUR VICTORY FROM THE VERY BEGINNING!

Today's Passage
In the end of the sabbath, as it began to dawn toward the first day of the week, came Mary Magdalene and the other Mary to see the sepulchre. And, behold, there was a great earthquake: for the angel of the Lord descended from heaven, and came and rolled back the stone from the door, and sat upon it. His countenance was like lightning, and his raiment white as snow: And for fear of him the keepers did shake, and became as dead men. And the angel answered and said unto the women, Fear not ye: for I know that ye seek Jesus, which was crucified. He is not here, for he is risen, as he said. Come, see the place where the Lord lay. And go quickly, and tell his disciples that he is risen from the dead; and, behold, he goeth before you into Galilee; there shall ye see him: lo, I have told you. And they departed quickly from the sepulchre with fear and great joy; and did run to bring his disciples word. And as they went to tell his disciples, behold, Jesus met them, saying, All hail. And they came and held him by the feet, and worshipped him (St. Matthew 28:1-9).

Today's Point To Practice
My favorite heavyweight boxer of all time is still Muhammed Ali. Don't get me wrong, I love Big George Foreman, Smokin' 'Joe Frazier, Iron Mike Tyson, Evander "The Real" Holyfield, and the list goes on. But there was something about Ali that I loved. Ali talked trash before every fight and was known for poetically predicting what round he would knock his opponent out. I loved it! In many instances, these became words of poetic prophecy because he would do exactly what he said he would do without fail and without compromise.

For this reason, many call Ali the GOAT. This is an acronym that stands for the Greatest Of All Time. Well, for believers in Christ Jesus, we can say that our GOAT is a LAMB! Jesus foretold His death and declared His resurrection before reaching the cross. Check out Matthew 16:21-23, Matthew 17:22-23, and Matthew 20:17-19. These are all references that show us our Lord telling us how the fight would go down and how He would get up!

In other words, He declared His victory before the fight took place!

Today's Push
Some people contend that talk is cheap. However, I beg to differ. The words that we speak shape the world that we live in. With this in mind, do not expect to talk about defeat and live in victory. It just won't happen in that manner.

WEEK 16: Help Me Handle It When What I Need Is an Upset

Declare your victory vocally, and watch God show it to you personally. God is faithful!

READ - Proverbs 18:21

Today's Prayer
Unto thee, O God, do I place my trust. Thankfully, I have entered your presence this day, and I have come saying, "Forgive me for speaking negatively with my mouth." Today, O Lord, I will only declare those things that you have promised in your Word. With this in heart, I speak victory over my life and live faithfully through your Son, my Savior, Jesus Christ.

In The Name of Jesus, Amen.

WEEK 16: Help Me Handle It When What I Need Is an Upset

Day 5

YOU SHOULD BE OUT, BUT YOU'RE STILL IN!

Today's Passage
In the end of the sabbath, as it began to dawn toward the first day of the week, came Mary Magdalene and the other Mary to see the sepulchre. And, behold, there was a great earthquake: for the angel of the Lord descended from heaven, and came and rolled back the stone from the door, and sat upon it. His countenance was like lightning, and his raiment white as snow: And for fear of him the keepers did shake, and became as dead men. And the angel answered and said unto the women, Fear not ye: for I know that ye seek Jesus, which was crucified. He is not here, for he is risen, as he said. Come, see the place where the Lord lay. And go quickly, and tell his disciples that he is risen from the dead; and, behold, he goeth before you into Galilee; there shall ye see him: lo, I have told you. And they departed quickly from the sepulchre with fear and great joy; and did run to bring his disciples word. And as they went to tell his disciples, behold, Jesus met them, saying, All hail. And they came and held him by the feet, and worshipped him (St. Matthew 28:1-9).

Today's Point To Practice
Growing up, we often played baseball in my neighborhood. It was a sport that we learned to play because all you needed was one tennis ball, one bat, a crushed can that could be a home plate, a couple of trees in your neighbor's yard, and maybe a parked car in the middle of the street, and it was on! You see, the crushed can would be home plate, the trees would be first base and third base, and the parked car in the middle of the street would be second base. It would be a game of champions!

The thing about baseball is when it's your turn to bat, all you will get is three strikes. After that, you are out. Someone else gets the bat, and you find yourself out of the game for the moment because you have struck out.

In this passage of study, the disciples of Jesus have struck out for sure. They have failed in so many ways it's not even funny. They have swung and missed at the mission of Jesus Christ, they have hit a long foul ball of both doubt and unbelief, and now Jesus has been crucified, and they are nowhere to be seen. By all practical standards, they should be out! But, in our passage today an angel shows up to make an announcement and He tells the woman at the tomb that Jesus is alive and to get the disciples and have them meet Jesus in Jerusalem!

WEEK 16: Help Me Handle It When What I Need Is an Upset

Isn't this the best news ever? They struck out and should be finished, but the Lord says even though you should be out, I still have you as in!

Today's Push

Take a look at your walk with the Lord. Consider this interrogative for just a moment: how many times have you struck out? I mean, you missed it completely. How many times have you failed God by being disobedient? Now, here's the most gracious news you will ever hear in your life: You should be out because you have had more than three strikes, but you are still in!

READ - Romans 5:20-21

Today's Prayer

Thank you, Jesus, for not giving up on me. I have made many mistakes, O Lord, yet you have kept me on your team and allowed me to continue walking with you despite my shortcomings, faults, and failures. God, I pray that people will look at me and discover how amazing your grace is.

In The Name of Jesus, Amen.

WEEK 16: Help Me Handle It When What I Need Is an Upset

Day 6

HELL HAPPENS BUT REMEMBER HEAVEN DOES TOO!

Today's Passage
In the end of the sabbath, as it began to dawn toward the first day of the week, came Mary Magdalene and the other Mary to see the sepulchre. And, behold, there was a great earthquake: for the angel of the Lord descended from heaven, and came and rolled back the stone from the door, and sat upon it. His countenance was like lightning, and his raiment white as snow: And for fear of him the keepers did shake, and became as dead men. And the angel answered and said unto the women, Fear not ye: for I know that ye seek Jesus, which was crucified. He is not here, for he is risen, as he said. Come, see the place where the Lord lay. And go quickly, and tell his disciples that he is risen from the dead; and, behold, he goeth before you into Galilee; there shall ye see him: lo, I have told you. And they departed quickly from the sepulchre with fear and great joy; and did run to bring his disciples word. And as they went to tell his disciples, behold, Jesus met them, saying, All hail. And they came and held him by the feet, and worshipped him (St. Matthew 28:1-9).

Today's Point To Practice
Hell is best defined as any place where the forces of darkness, spirits of evil, and the will of the enemy can have total control. When this definition is considered, we must conclude that hell is not just a fiery place that exists for the afterlife of those who did not believe. Hell happens every day, everywhere, all of the time.

When Jesus was dying on that cross, God was very much in complete control, but hell broke loose in mad fashion. It was so bad it appeared that hell became victorious for a few days. The news within the text that builds our faith and strengthens believers from the inside out is this: just like hell breaks loose, so does heaven!

When heaven breaks loose the bound go free, the guilty find grace, the miserable gain mercy and the deceased are raised from the dead! This is what took place on Easter Sunday morning! Heaven broke loose and turned what looked like midnight into the brilliance of day!

Today's Push
Receive this message right now in faith and let it remain with you until the day you meet the Lord face-to-face; whenever God shows up, heaven just broke loose!

READ - St. John 20:19-29

WEEK 16: Help Me Handle It When What I Need Is an Upset

Today's Prayer

Lord Jesus, I have just one request of you right now. Please show up amid every circumstance and condition where hell tries to destroy me. Let heaven break loose on my job, in my home, in my resources, and in my heart. Lord, let heaven reign, is my prayer.

In The Name of Jesus, Amen.

WEEK 16: Help Me Handle It When What I Need Is an Upset

Day 7

YOUR SETBACK IS ONE THING, BUT YOUR UPSET IS ANOTHER!

Today's Passage

In the end of the sabbath, as it dawned toward the first day of the week, Mary Magdalene and the other Mary came to see the sepulchre. And, behold, there was a great earthquake: for the angel of the Lord descended from heaven, and came and rolled back the stone from the door, and sat upon it. His countenance was like lightning, and his raiment white as snow: And for fear of him, the keepers did shake and became as dead men. And the angel answered and said unto the women, Fear not ye: for I know that ye seek Jesus, which was crucified. He is not here, for he is risen, as he said. Come, see the place where the Lord lay. And go quickly, and tell his disciples that he is risen from the dead; and, behold, he goeth before you into Galilee; there shall ye see him: lo, I have told you. And they departed quickly from the sepulchre with fear and great joy; and did run to bring his disciples word. And as they went to tell his disciples, behold, Jesus met them, saying, All hail. And they came and held him by the feet, and worshipped him (St. Matthew 28:1-9).

Today's Point To Practice

If you are a sports enthusiast like me you have come to understand and even expect your team to have some setbacks during the course of the game. A penalty that cost your team fifteen yards, a foul in the paint was called a tech, a player ejected from the game for something flagrant, and the list goes on. There are times when even the strongest teams see setbacks. However, an upset is a whole different story. An upset says you were not supposed to win from the beginning. The odds were stacked against you. It would be a miracle for you to win, and everyone knows it.

In our study passage for the week, we see the world's most incredible upset! The Roman Empire is against Jesus because, in their minds, they already have a king. The Jews hated Him because He was a self-proclaimed ruler who broke all of the rules and said that He could forgive sins. These two earthly forces come together to get rid of this Jewish revolutionary called Jesus once and for all. They strip Him, beat Him, mock Him, and nail Him to a tree while He is still alive. He dies, and they celebrate.

It appears that all hope is gone. And the upset starts to take place! Death can't hold Him, the grave can't keep Him, the nails could not destroy Him, and the cross could not defeat Him! He who was dead is resurrected!

WEEK 16: Help Me Handle It When What I Need Is an Upset

Today's Push

You should expect an upset if your problem is not bigger than Jesus nailed to the cross! God has the power, the ability, and the authority to turn your situation around! When you cannot handle it, God can and will!

READ - St. Matthew 28:16-20

Today's Prayer

On a day like today, I choose to remember your resurrection and shout, "Thank you, Jesus!" I bless your name today, O God because there are so many times in life when the odds are stacked against me, and because you are with me, I come out on top! Thank you, Jesus. You have risen from the grave, and you alone are Lord.

In The Name of Jesus, Amen.

Antioch Missionary Baptist Church
3920 W. Cardinal Drive Beaumont, TX 77705
Dr. John R. Adolph, Pastor
Website www.antiochbmt.org
FaceBook: Antioch Missionary Baptist Church
IG: @antiochbmt

Worship Service
Every Sunday at 8:00 am & 10:00 am
Virtual and Personal
Website: www.antiochbmt.org
YouTube: John R. Adolph Ministries LLC.

War Room Prayer Call
Every Wednesday at 7:00 am
YouTube: John R. Adolph Ministries LLC.
Dial 667-770-1807

Bible Study
Every Thursday at 6:00 pm
Virtual and Personal
Website: www.antiochbmt.org
YouTube: John R. Adolph Ministries LLC.

John R. Adolph Ministries LLC.
The Message. The Ministry. The Man.
Website: www.jradolph.com

YouTube: John R. Adolph Ministries LLC.

FaceBook: John R. Adolph Ministries LLC.

IG: @iamjradolph

Other Books by John R. Adolph
Other Books and Articles by John R. Adolph

I'm Changing the Game
Not Without A Fight
I'm Coming Out of This
Just Stick to the Script
Victorious Christian Living Volume I
Victorious Christian Living Volume II
Let Me Encourage You Volume I
Let Me Encourage You Volume II
The Him Book
Marriage Is For Losers
Celibacy is for Fools
Victory: Ten Fundamental Beliefs That Eradicate Defeat in the Life of a Christian
Better Together
Based On A True Story
Back To The Table

Articles-Zondervan Press
He Loves Me, He Loves Me, He Loves Me
I'm Certain That He Loves Me
His Love Made The Difference
God's Mind Is Made Up, He Loves You

To purchase additional copies of this book or other books by Dr Adolph
or visit Amazon.com our bookstore website at:
www.advbookstore.com

Orlando, Florida, USA
"we bring dreams to life"™
www.advbookstore.com

www.ingramcontent.com/pod-product-compliance
Lightning Source LLC
Chambersburg PA
CBHW081328190426
43193CB00044B/2888